Better Homes and Gardens®

SKILLET MEALS

HOUGHTON MIFFLIN HARCOURT
BOSTON • NEW YORK

BETTER HOMES AND GARDENS® SKILLET MEALS

Editor: Jan Miller
Project Editor: Annie Peterson, Waterbury Publications, Inc.
Contributing Editor: Tricia Bergman, Waterbury Publications, Inc.
Contributing Copy Editor and Proofreader: Carrie Truesdell, Terri Fredrickson
Test Kitchen Director: Lynn Blanchard
Test Kitchen Product Supervisor: Juliana Hale
Test Kitchen Home Economists: Sarah Brekke, Linda Brewer, Carla Christian, Sammy Mila, Jill Moberly, Colleen Weeden, Lori Wilson
Contributing Photographers: Waterbury Publications, Inc.
Contributing Stylists: Charlie Worthington
Administrative Assistants: Barb Allen, Marlene Todd

SPECIAL INTEREST MEDIA

Editorial Leader: Doug Kouma
Editorial Director, Food: Jennifer Dorland Darling

HOUGHTON MIFFLIN HARCOURT

Editorial Director: Cindy Kitchel
Executive Editor, Brands: Anne Ficklen
Editorial Associate: Molly Aronica
Managing Editor: Marina Padakis Lowry
Art Director: Tai Blanche
Production Director: Tom Hyland

WATERBURY PUBLICATIONS, INC.

Design Director: Ken Carlson
Associate Design Director: Doug Samuelson
Production Assistant: Mindy Samuelson

Library of Congress Cataloging-in-Publication Data is available.

ISBN 978-0-544-80087-8 (pbk)
ISBN 978-0-544-80091-5 (ebk)

Book design by Waterbury Publications, Inc., Des Moines, Iowa.

Printed in China

SCP 10 9 8 7 6 5 4

4500710943

Our seal assures you that every recipe in *Better Homes and Gardens® Skillet Meals* has been tested in the Better Homes and Gardens® Test Kitchen. This means that each recipe is practical and reliable and meets our high standards of taste appeal. We guarantee your satisfaction with this book for as long as you own it.

Pictured on front cover:
Chicken, Bacon, and Veggie Skillet , page 148

Pictured on back cover:
Cheesy Ham Chilaquiles, page 51; Skillet Calzone, page 140; Blackberry Clafouti, page 274

HOW TO USE THIS BOOK

Look for these icons throughout this cookbook, indicating the recipe is low in fat and calories, ready in 30 minutes or less, or cast-iron-friendly.

♥

ENTRÈES
Calories 425 or less
Fat 15 grams or less

APPETIZERS & PARTY FOODS + SIDES
Calories 175 or less
Fat 5 grams or less

DESSERTS
Calories 200 or less
Fat 8 grams or less

30 MINUTES OR LESS

CAST-IRON FRIENDLY

CONTENTS

SKILLET 101

SKILLET COOKING

WITH A LARGE SURFACE AREA AND LOW SIDES, THIS KITCHEN STAPLE IS THE PERFECT TOOL FOR SEARING FOODS AND SIMMERING AWAY MOISTURE.

THE SECRET TO BROWNING is using a heavy-bottom pan. Don't overcrowd the pan; overcrowding promotes steaming instead of browning. Work in batches if browning more than 1½ pounds of ground meat or more than four chops, steaks, or chicken breasts. Cook a single layer of food at one time and allow space for liquid to evaporate.

THE SECRET TO EVEN COOKING is preheating. Always heat a pan before adding the food. Adding ingredients to a pan before it's reached medium to medium-high heat will cause food to stick to the pan and make for uneven cooking.

WHAT DOES SAUTÉ MEAN It is a method of cooking food quickly over high heat in a shallow pan using a little fat. The word comes from the French term *sauter*, which means "to jump." Chefs often shake the pan instead of stirring, making the food jump.

WHAT SIZE PAN The Better Homes and Gardens® Test Kitchen uses small, medium, large, and extra-large when referring to sizes of skillets (see below).

CAST-IRON COOKING

THE ROCK-SOLID RELIABILITY OF CAST IRON HAS BEEN FEEDING AMERICANS FOR CENTURIES. HERE ARE TIPS FOR SEASONING, STORING, AND MAINTAINING CAST IRON.

WHAT IS SEASONING Seasoning involves baking a thin layer of oil onto the surface of cast iron. To check if your skillet needs to be seasoned, look at its surface. If it has a smooth, even sheen and water beads off it, it's seasoned. If the surface is dull, it needs to be seasoned. If not well seasoned, acidic food can react with the metal and give an off-flavor to food. In general, avoid long-simmered acidic food, particularly tomato sauce, but a short simmer won't harm your food or your pan.

TO SEASON CAST IRON preheat your oven to 350°F. Wash the pan with hot water and a plastic scrub brush (no soap). Rinse well and dry thoroughly. If there are any stuck-on food bits, scour the skillet with coarse salt, then rinse and dry well. Using a paper towel, rub a thin layer of vegetable oil all over the skillet, inside and out. Place a layer of foil on the bottom rack of your oven to catch any drips, then preheat it to 350°F. Place the skillet, upside down, on a rack above the foil. Bake for 1 hour. Turn oven off and allow the skillet to cool completely in the oven.

TO MAINTAIN A SEASONED SKILLET wash it only with a plastic scrub brush and hot water while the skillet is still warm. Dry it thoroughly, then rub a few drops of vegetable oil on the inside of the skillet before storing.

TO STORE CAST IRON place it in a dry spot, such as on paper or a cloth, without a lid. This will allow air to circulate around the skillet and prevent rust.

For an easy reference, see the "Cast-Iron Friendly Recipes" index, page 3.

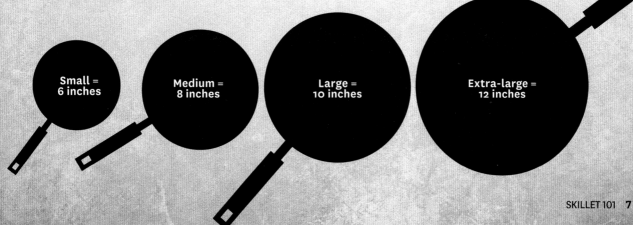

Small = 6 inches

Medium = 8 inches

Large = 10 inches

Extra-large = 12 inches

PICKING A PAN

ALL SKILLETS ARE NOT CREATED EQUALLY. WHETHER YOU WANT AN EASY-CLEAN SKILLET THAT RESISTS STICKING OR A HEAVY-DUTY PAN FOR FRYING AND SEARING, USE THIS GUIDE TO CHOOSE THE RIGHT PAN FOR YOUR NEEDS AND LEARN HOW TO CARE FOR IT PROPERLY.

	DESCRIPTION	CLEANING & CARE	PRICE
CAST IRON	Cast-iron pans are very heavy and sturdy. They absorb, conduct, and retain heat well.	Cast iron requires seasoning before use. Seasoning creates a natural nonstick finish that prevents the iron from reacting with food. Don't use soapy water to clean this type of pan. Simply wipe it out with paper towels or use water to wash; immediately dry thoroughly to prevent rust. (See page 7 for more about caring for cast iron.)	Available at kitchen stores for $20–$50.
COPPER	Typically lined with stainless steel, these pans are very heavy and sturdy. They are perhaps the best for conducting heat.	These skillets require polishing to keep the blue-green pigment called verdigris from discoloring the pan and interacting with food. If you invest in copper and use your copper pan frequently, replace the lining about every 10 years.	Available at specialty kitchen stores for $75–$400.
STAINLESS STEEL	Stainless steel has poor heat conductivity compared with other materials. For better heating, some manufacturers insert a core of aluminum or copper, which is called tri-ply.	Stainless steel is a strong material that doesn't scratch or dent easily. It doesn't react with acidic foods, and it's very easy to clean.	Widely available at discount and department stores for around $20; tri-ply runs $50–$200.
ALUMINUM	These sturdy pans are good heat conductors. The heavier the pan, the more evenly it will cook.	Choose aluminum cookware that is anodized aluminum or coated with a nonstick finish to avoid acidic foods reacting with the metal, discoloring the food. It's typically chip- and scratch-resistant. **Note:** Use nonmetal utensils to avoid scratching the pan.	Available at discount and department stores for $15–$85.
CERAMIC NONSTICK	The pan is made of aluminum, and the inside is coated with nonstick ceramic. It conducts heat well.	Ceramic nonstick pans combine the best of everything. The nonreactive surface is easy to clean. Cool completely before washing. **Note:** Not all ceramic nonstick skillets are safe for use in the oven. Use nonmetal utensils to avoid scratching the pan.	Available at kitchen stores for $20–$50.

OVEN-GOING OR STOVE TOP ONLY? Most skillets are oven-safe, but not all. All-metal pans—including the handle—can go in the oven. It's when you add the enamel or nonstick coating that it becomes debatable. Some are safe up to a certain temperature. If you're unsure, check with the manufacturer before using a skillet in the oven. You can risk ruining your skillet and your oven.

NO RECIPE NEEDED

MAKE A PAN SAUCE Remove cooked chicken or meat pieces from the hot pan. Add a liquid (wine or broth) and desired seasonings to the pan. Cook and stir to scrape up browned bits from the bottom of the pan. Bring to boiling. Boil gently until sauce is reduced to the desired consistency.

ADD RICHNESS To further flavor and thicken the sauce, whisk in a couple tablespoons of whipping cream and/or butter, stirring after each addition.

APPETIZERS & PARTY FOODS

SPICY APPLE-GLAZED MEATBALLS

PREP 20 minutes

STAND 10 minutes

COOK 6 minutes per batch

1 egg

¼ cup milk

2 slices white or whole wheat bread, torn

1 lb. 85% lean ground beef

4 cloves garlic, minced

½ tsp. freshly ground black pepper

¼ tsp. salt

½ tsp. cayenne pepper

1 Tbsp. vegetable oil

1 cup apple juice or pear nectar

¼ cup reduced-sodium soy sauce

3 Tbsp. packed brown sugar

1½ tsp. cornstarch

1 tsp. ground ginger

6 green onions, chopped

TO MAKE THESE MEATBALLS IN ADVANCE, PLACE THE COOKED MEATBALLS IN A SINGLE LAYER ON A BAKING SHEET. FREEZE THE MEATBALLS OVERNIGHT, THEN TRANSFER THEM TO A RESEALABLE PLASTIC BAG. STORE IN THE FREEZER FOR UP TO TWO MONTHS. TO USE, THAW THE MEATBALLS IN THE REFRIGERATOR OR MICROWAVE, AND PREPARE THE SAUCE JUST BEFORE SERVING.

1. For meatballs, in a bowl whisk together egg and milk; add bread. Let stand 10 minutes or just until bread is softened. Add beef, garlic, black pepper, salt, and ¼ tsp. of the cayenne pepper. Mix thoroughly. Shape into 48 meatballs.

2. In an extra-large skillet cook meatballs, half at a time, in hot oil over medium heat 6 minutes, or until done (160°F), turning occasionally. Remove meatballs from skillet; drain off fat.

3. For glaze, in a bowl combine apple juice, soy sauce, brown sugar, cornstarch, ginger, and the remaining ¼ tsp. cayenne pepper. Add to skillet; cook and stir until glaze is thickened and bubbly. Cook and stir 2 minutes more. Return meatballs to skillet and heat through. Transfer to a serving dish and top with green onions. **MAKES 12 SERVINGS.**

PER 4 MEATBALLS *143 cal., 8 g fat (3 g sat. fat), 42 mg chol., 297 mg sodium, 10 g carb., 0 g fiber, 9 g pro.*

SRIRACHA PORK MEATBALLS

PREP 30 minutes

COOK 20 minutes

1 egg, lightly beaten

¼ cup fine dry bread crumbs

¼ cup sliced green onions

1 clove garlic, minced

1 tsp. grated fresh ginger

3 Tbsp. reduced-sodium soy sauce

2 Tbsp. sriracha sauce

1 lb. ground pork

1 Tbsp. vegetable oil

¾ cup ketchup

¼ cup packed brown sugar

1 Tbsp. toasted sesame oil

1 Tbsp. rice vinegar

2 Tbsp. chopped fresh cilantro

2 tsp. sesame seeds, toasted*

STICK A COCKTAIL PICK INTO EACH OF THESE ASIAN-STYLE MEATBALLS AND SERVE THEM STRAIGHT FROM THE SKILLET AT YOUR NEXT PARTY.

1. In a bowl combine egg, bread crumbs, green onions, garlic, ginger, and 1 Tbsp. each of the soy sauce and sriracha. Add ground pork; mix well. Shape into 18 meatballs. In a large skillet cook meatballs, half at a time, in hot vegetable oil over medium heat 5 minutes, turning occasionally. Remove meatballs from skillet; drain off fat.

2. Meanwhile, for sauce, in a bowl stir together ketchup, brown sugar, remaining 2 Tbsp. soy sauce, remaining 1 Tbsp. sriracha, the sesame oil, and rice vinegar. Add to skillet and stir over medium heat until bubbly, scraping up any browned bits. Return meatballs to skillet. Reduce heat; cover and cook 5 minutes. Uncover; cook 5 minutes more or until meatballs are done (160°F), turning occasionally. Sprinkle with cilantro and sesame seeds. **MAKES 18 SERVINGS.**

*Toasting Nuts, Seeds, and Coconut To toast whole nuts or large pieces, spread them in a shallow pan. Bake in a 350°F oven 5 to 10 minutes, shaking the pan once or twice. Toast coconut the same way, but watch closely to avoid burning it. Toast finely chopped or ground nuts or seeds in a dry skillet over medium heat. Stir often so nuts don't burn.

PER MEATBALL *107 cal., 6 g fat (2 g sat. fat), 27 mg chol., 237 mg sodium, 8 g carb., 0 g fiber, 5 g pro.*

SAUSAGES IN BOURBON-HONEY BARBECUE SAUCE

PREP 10 minutes

COOK 15 minutes

1 18-oz. bottle barbecue sauce (1⅔ cups)

¼ cup bourbon

2 Tbsp. Dijon-style mustard

2 14-oz. links smoked sausage, sliced ½ inch thick

Bite-size pieces sweet pepper, fresh pineapple, and/or dill pickle chips

CUT THE FAT IN THIS FAVORITE APPETIZER BY USING CHICKEN OR TURKEY SAUSAGES. SPICE UP THE RECIPE BY USING ANDOUILLE SMOKED SAUSAGE.

1. In a large skillet combine barbecue sauce, bourbon, and mustard. Cook and stir over medium heat until bubbly. Stir in smoked sausage slices. Cook, covered, over medium-low heat 15 minutes or until heated through, stirring occasionally.

2. Serve sausages with short skewers and sweet pepper, pineapple, and/or pickles. **MAKES 16 SERVINGS.**

PER SERVING *223 cal., 14 g fat (5 g sat. fat), 30 mg chol., 820 mg sodium, 15 g carb., 1 g fiber, 6 g pro.*

CAJUN TURKEY SLIDERS WITH SPICY REMOULADE

PREP 25 minutes

COOK 18 minutes

- 2 Tbsp. vegetable oil
- 1 medium red sweet pepper, cut into thin strips
- 1 medium yellow sweet pepper, cut into thin strips
- 1 medium onion, cut into thin wedges
- 1½ lb. ground turkey
- ¼ cup chopped green onions
- 2 tsp. Cajun seasoning
- 1 tsp. hot pepper sauce
- ½ tsp. salt
- ¼ tsp. black pepper
- 12 whole wheat cocktail buns, split and toasted
- 2 Tbsp. Old Bay seasoning or seafood seasoning
- 1 recipe Spicy Remoulade

REMOULADE IS A CLASSIC FRENCH SAUCE THAT COMBINES MAYONNAISE, MUSTARD, PICKLES, CAPERS, AND FRESH HERBS. THE VERSION THAT TOPS THESE COCKTAIL-SIZE BURGERS HAS A SPICY KICK FROM THE ADDITION OF HOT SAUCE.

1. In an extra-large skillet heat 1 Tbsp. of the oil over medium-low heat. Add sweet peppers and onion; cook 10 minutes or until very soft. Remove from skillet; keep warm.

2. In a bowl combine the next six ingredients (through black pepper); mix well. Shape into 12 patties slightly larger than the buns. Generously sprinkle both sides with Old Bay seasoning.

3. In the same skillet heat remaining 1 Tbsp. oil over medium heat. Add patties; cook 8 minutes or until done (165°F), turning once.

4. Serve patties on buns with sweet pepper mixture and Spicy Remoulade. **MAKES 12 SLIDERS.**

SPICY REMOULADE In a bowl combine 1 cup mayonnaise; ¼ cup pickle relish; 2 Tbsp. capers, drained; 1 Tbsp. Creole or spicy brown mustard; 1 Tbsp. snipped fresh Italian parsley; 2 tsp. hot pepper sauce; and 1 tsp. lemon juice.

PER SLIDER *334 cal., 23 g fat (4 g sat. fat), 52 mg chol., 878 mg sodium, 20 g carb., 3 g fiber, 13 g pro.*

4 WAYS WITH WINGS

12 chicken wings (about 2½ lb.)

2 Tbsp. vegetable oil

1 recipe Wing Sauce

Thinly sliced green onions (optional)

BROWN CHICKEN WINGS TO CRISPY, GOLDEN PERFECTION, THEN SIMMER THEM IN ONE OF FOUR LIP-SMACKING, ASIAN-INSPIRED SAUCES. SAVE TIME BY PURCHASING WING PIECES THAT HAVE ALREADY BEEN CUT APART.

1. Cut off and discard tips of chicken wings. Cut wings at joints to form 24 pieces. In an extra-large skillet heat oil over medium-high heat. Add wings; cook 10 minutes or until browned, turning once. Drain off fat.

2. Pour desired Wing Sauce over chicken wings. Simmer, covered, 5 minutes. Simmer, uncovered, 10 to 15 minutes more or until chicken is no longer pink and sauce is slightly thickened, stirring occasionally. Transfer to a serving platter. If desired, sprinkle with green onions. **MAKES 12 SERVINGS.**

SPICY PEKING WING SAUCE In a bowl combine ½ cup each plum sauce, dry white wine, and reduced-sodium chicken broth; ⅓ cup thinly sliced fresh ginger; and 2 Tbsp. sriracha sauce.

SHANGHAI MARKET WING SAUCE In a bowl combine ½ cup dry white wine; ⅓ cup thinly sliced fresh ginger; ¼ cup reduced-sodium soy sauce; 2 Tbsp. each hoisin sauce, frozen orange juice concentrate, and honey; 1 tsp. five-spice powder; and 1 clove garlic, thinly sliced.

PINEAPPLE TERIYAKI WING SAUCE In a bowl combine ½ cup reduced-sodium soy sauce, ½ cup sake or dry white wine, ⅓ cup unsweetened pineapple juice, 2 Tbsp. each honey and thinly sliced fresh ginger, and 1 clove garlic, thinly sliced.

BANGKOK CHILE WING SAUCE Seed, peel, and cut up 1 medium mango. In a food processor or blender process or blend mango until smooth. In a bowl combine pureed mango, ½ of a 14-oz. can unsweetened light coconut milk, 1 Tbsp. each sriracha sauce and lime juice, and 1 tsp. kosher salt.

PER SERVING *169 cal., 10 g fat (3 g sat. fat), 39 mg chol., 176 mg sodium, 7 g carb., 0 g fiber, 10 g pro.*

ORANGE SHRIMP AND AVOCADO CROSTINI

PREP 15 minutes

BROIL 2 minutes

COOK 3 minutes

16 fresh or frozen large shrimp

1 orange

1 large ripe avocado, halved, seeded, and peeled

½ tsp. salt

⅛ tsp. black pepper

2 tsp. snipped fresh Italian parsley

1 tsp. snipped fresh chives

16 ½-inch slices baguette-style French bread

2 Tbsp. olive oil

2 cloves garlic, minced

¼ tsp. crushed red pepper

CUT DOWN ON PREP TIME BY PURCHASING SHRIMP THAT HAS ALREADY BEEN PEELED AND DEVEINED. IF YOU LIKE, ADD A LITTLE EXTRA HEAT BY TOPPING EACH CROSTINI WITH ADDITIONAL CRUSHED RED PEPPER.

1. Thaw shrimp, if frozen. Peel and devein shrimp. Rinse shrimp; pat dry with paper towels. Remove 1 tsp. zest and 2 tsp. juice from the orange.

2. Preheat broiler. In a bowl combine avocado, orange juice, ¼ tsp. of the salt, and the black pepper; mash gently. Stir in parsley and chives.

3. Arrange bread slices on a large baking sheet. Lightly brush top of slices with 1 Tbsp. of the olive oil. Broil 3 to 4 inches from the heat 2 minutes or until toasted, turning once.

4. In a large nonstick skillet heat remaining 1 Tbsp. olive oil over medium-high heat. Add shrimp, garlic, crushed red pepper, and remaining ¼ tsp. salt. Cook and stir 3 minutes or until shrimp are opaque. Stir in orange zest.

5. Spread avocado mixture onto crostini. Top with shrimp. If desired, sprinkle with additional parsley and chives. **MAKES 16 SERVINGS.**

PER CROSTINI *69 cal., 3 g fat (0 g sat. fat), 17 mg chol., 143 mg sodium, 6 g carb., 1 g fiber, 3 g pro.*

INDIAN-SPICED SWEET POTATO FRITTERS

PREP 15 minutes

COOK 8 minutes per batch

⅔ cup plain whole milk yogurt

2 Tbsp. snipped fresh cilantro

½ tsp. lime zest

⅛ tsp. salt

Dash cayenne pepper

1 lb. sweet potatoes, peeled and coarsely shredded

¼ cup sliced green onions

½ cup all-purpose flour

1¼ tsp. garam masala

½ tsp. baking powder

½ tsp. salt

¼ tsp. ground cumin

⅛ tsp. black pepper

1 egg, lightly beaten

2 Tbsp. canola oil

Lime wedges (optional)

FOR THE BEST FLAVOR, CHOOSE SMALL TO MEDIUM SWEET POTATOES FOR THESE FRITTERS. LARGER ONES TEND TO BE LESS SWEET AND MORE STARCHY.

1. For yogurt sauce, in a bowl stir together the first five ingredients (through cayenne pepper).
2. In a bowl combine sweet potatoes and green onions. Add the next six ingredients (through black pepper); toss to coat. Stir in egg until combined.
3. In a large nonstick skillet heat 2 tsp. of the oil over medium heat. Working in batches, drop batter by slightly rounded tablespoons into the hot skillet. Use a spatula to flatten into ½-inch-thick patties. Cook 4 to 5 minutes per side or until browned. Keep fritters warm in a 200°F oven while cooking remaining batter, adding more oil as needed (you should have about 18 fritters).

4. Serve fritters with yogurt sauce and, if desired, lime wedges. **MAKES 18 SERVINGS.**
PER FRITTER *58 cal., 2 g fat (0 g sat. fat), 12 mg chol., 175 mg sodium, 8 g carb., 1 g fiber, 1 g pro.*

BACON-CHEDDAR POTATO DIP

PREP 30 minutes
COOK 15 minutes
BAKE 20 minutes at 425°F
BROIL 1 minute

2¼ lb. Yukon gold or other yellow-flesh potatoes, peeled and quartered

4 slices hickory- or applewood-smoked bacon

1 10-oz. container cream cheese for cooking

1 cup shredded sharp cheddar cheese (4 oz.)

½ cup sour cream

¼ cup chopped green onions

¼ tsp. garlic salt

Sour cream-and-onion-flavor potato chips and/or sweet pepper wedges

BUTTERY YELLOW YUKON GOLD POTATOES—THE IDEAL POTATO VARIETY FOR MASHED POTATOES—ENSURE A MOIST, SMOOTH TEXTURE IN THIS DIP.

1. Preheat oven to 425°F. In a large saucepan cook potatoes, covered, in enough boiling lightly salted water to cover 15 to 20 minutes or until tender; drain.

2. Meanwhile, in a large skillet cook bacon over medium heat until crisp. Drain on paper towels. Crumble bacon; reserve 1 Tbsp. for topping.

3. In a large bowl combine remaining crumbled bacon, cream cheese, ¾ cup of the cheddar cheese, the sour cream, green onions, and garlic salt. Press cooked potatoes through a ricer* onto cheese mixture; stir gently to combine. Spoon potato mixture into a generously greased medium oven-going skillet.

4. Bake 20 to 25 minutes or until heated through and a thermometer registers 160°F. Remove from oven.

5. Preheat broiler. Top dip with remaining ¼ cup cheddar cheese and reserved 1 Tbsp. crumbled bacon. Broil 4 to 5 inches from the heat 1 to 2 minutes or until cheese is melted and bubbly. Serve dip with potato chips. **MAKES 24 SERVINGS.**

BACON-BLUE CHEESE POTATO DIP Prepare as directed, except substitute ¾ cup crumbled blue cheese (3 oz.) for the cheddar cheese in the potato mixture, and ¼ cup crumbled blue cheese (1 oz.) for the cheddar cheese in the topping. Serve with barbecue-flavor potato chips or celery sticks.

*Tip If you don't have a potato ricer, mash potatoes with a potato masher until fluffy.

Slow Cooker Directions Prepare potato mixture as directed through Step 3, except spoon mixture into a 1½- or 2-quart slow cooker. Cover and cook on low 2 hours or until heated through (160°F). Top with remaining cheese and reserved bacon. Serve with potato chips.

PER SERVING *79 cal., 5 g fat (3 g sat. fat), 14 mg chol., 127 mg sodium, 6 g carb., 1 g fiber, 3 g pro.*

PIZZA SUPREME DIP

START TO FINISH 35 minutes

8 oz. bulk Italian sausage

½ cup chopped onion

1 clove garlic, minced

1 15-oz. can pizza sauce

1 cup thinly sliced, cooked turkey pepperoni or mini pepperoni, or chopped Canadian-style bacon

1 cup coarsely chopped fresh portobello or cremini mushrooms

½ cup coarsely chopped green sweet pepper

¼ cup sliced pitted ripe olives

¾ cup shredded four-cheese pizza cheese (3 oz.)

1 recipe Pizza Chips, bagel chips, and/or toasted baguette-style French bread slices

OPT FOR A HEAVY OVEN-SAFE SKILLET FOR THIS PIZZA-INSPIRED DIP. THE HEAVIER THE SKILLET, THE LONGER IT WILL MAINTAIN ITS HEAT AND KEEP THE DIP WARM AND DELICIOUS.

1. Preheat broiler. In a generously greased medium oven-going skillet, cook sausage, onion, and garlic over medium-high heat until sausage is browned. Drain off fat.

2. Stir in pizza sauce, pepperoni, mushrooms, sweet pepper, and olives. Cook over medium heat until bubbly, stirring occasionally. Top with cheese.

3. Broil 3 to 4 inches from the heat 2 to 3 minutes or just until cheese starts to brown. Serve with Pizza Chips. **MAKES 16 SERVINGS.**

PIZZA CHIPS Preheat broiler. Stack four 8-inch pizza crusts (such as Boboli brand); cut stack into eight wedges. Arrange wedges in a single layer on an extra-large baking sheet. Broil 4 inches from the heat 4 minutes or until wedges are lightly toasted, turning once. Cool. Makes 32 chips.

Slow Cooker Directions Prepare as directed in Step 1, using any medium skillet to cook sausage mixture. Stir in pizza sauce, pepperoni, mushrooms, sweet pepper, and olives. Transfer pepperoni mixture to a 1½-quart slow cooker. Sprinkle with cheese. Cover and cook on low 4 hours or on high 2 hours or until bubbly. Serve with Pizza Chips.

PER SERVING *104 cal., 7 g fat (3 g sat. fat), 24 mg chol., 337 mg sodium, 4 g carb., 1 g fiber, 6 g pro.*

HOT CHIPPED BEEF DIP

PREP 15 minutes

BAKE 20 minutes at 400°F

- 1 8-oz. pkg. cream cheese, softened
- 1 8-oz. carton sour cream
- ¼ cup milk
- 1 Tbsp. cream-style prepared horseradish
- 1 tsp. Worcestershire sauce
- 2 2.5-oz. pkg. sliced dried beef, coarsely chopped
- ½ cup finely chopped red onion
- ½ cup finely chopped celery
- 2 tsp. snipped fresh dil weed or ½ tsp. dried dill weed

   Cornichons and mini rye toasts

ALSO REFERRED TO AS DRIED BEEF, CHIPPED BEEF IS WAFER-THIN SLICES OF BEEF THAT HAVE BEEN SALTED, PRESSED, SMOKED, AND DRIED. DRIED BEEF LENDS AN INTENSE SAVORY FLAVOR TO THIS HOT PARTY DIP.

1. Preheat oven to 400°F. In a bowl beat cream cheese on medium until fluffy. Add sour cream, milk, horseradish, and Worcestershire sauce until combined. Stir in dried beef, onion, celery, and dill. Transfer dip to a generously greased medium oven-going skillet.

2. Bake 20 minutes or until dip is bubbly. Top with additional fresh dill. Serve with cornichons and mini rye toasts. **MAKES 28 SERVINGS.**

Slow Cooker Directions Prepare beef mixture as directed, except transfer mixture to a 1½-quart slow cooker. Cover and cook on low 3 hours or until heated through (if no heat setting is available, cook for 2 hours). Stir before serving.

PER SERVING *56 cal., 5 g fat (3 g sat. fat), 17 mg chol., 182 mg sodium, 1 g carb., 0 g fiber, 2 g pro.*

CHIPOTLE CHORIZO AND BEAN DIP

PREP 30 minutes

BAKE 15 minutes at 450°F

- 8 oz. uncooked chorizo sausage, casings removed if present
- ½ cup chopped onion
- 2 cloves garlic, minced
- 1 15-oz. can black beans, rinsed and drained
- 1 14.5-oz. can diced tomatoes, undrained
- ¼ cup snipped fresh cilantro
- 1 to 2 tsp. chopped canned chipotle peppers in adobo sauce
- 1 15-oz. can pinto beans, rinsed and drained
- ½ cup shredded Monterey Jack cheese with jalapeño peppers (2 oz.)

  Lime wedges

  Tortilla chips

A TRIPLE DOSE OF HEAT FROM THE MEXICAN CHORIZO SAUSAGE, CHIPOTLE PEPPERS, AND PEPPER-JACK CHEESE MAKES THIS DIP PERFECT FOR SPICY FOOD FANS. TO TAME THE HEAT A BIT, SWAP OUT THE SPICY CHEESE WITH PLAIN MONTEREY JACK.

1. Preheat oven to 450°F. In a generously greased medium oven-going skillet cook sausage, onion, and garlic over medium-high heat until sausage is browned. Remove from skillet; drain on paper towels.

2. In a bowl combine black beans, tomatoes, cilantro, chipotle peppers, and sausage mixture. In another bowl mash pinto beans; spread in the skillet. Top with tomato mixture and sprinkle with cheese.

3. Bake 15 minutes or until cheese is golden and dip is bubbly. Serve with lime wedges and tortilla chips and sprinkle with additional cilantro. **MAKES 16 SERVINGS.**

Slow Cooker Directions Prepare recipe as directed, using any medium skillet. Spread mashed beans in a 1½-quart slow cooker; top with tomato mixture and sprinkle with cheese. Cover and cook on low 4 hours or on high 2 hours or until bubbly.

PER SERVING *127 cal., 7 g fat (3 g sat. fat), 16 mg chol., 398 mg sodium, 11 g carb., 3 g fiber, 8 g pro.*

CHEESY SKILLET ARTICHOKE DIP

PREP 30 minutes
RISE 1 hour
BAKE 30 minutes at 375°F
STAND 10 minutes

1 15- to 16-oz. pkg. frozen white dinner rolls, thawed (12 rolls)

1 8-oz. pkg. cream cheese, softened

1 8-oz. carton sour cream

¼ cup milk

1 8-oz. pkg. shredded Italian-blend cheeses (2 cups)

2 14-oz. cans artichoke hearts, drained and chopped

3 cups choppped fresh baby spinach

½ cup sliced green onions

2 cloves garlic, minced

1 Tbsp. butter, melted

1 Tbsp. grated Parmesan cheese

TO MAKE THIS DIP AHEAD OF TIME, PREPARE AS DIRECTED IN STEP 2. COVER THE SURFACE OF THE DIP WITH PLASTIC WRAP. CHILL UP TO 4 HOURS BEFORE BAKING. PREPARE THE ROLLS AND BAKE AS DIRECTED.

1. Divide each roll into two portions. Shape each portion into a small ball, pulling edges under to make a smooth top. Place rolls 2 to 3 inches apart on floured parchment or waxed paper. Cover; let rise in a warm place until nearly double in size (1 to 1½ hours).
2. Preheat oven to 375°F. In an extra-large bowl beat cream cheese on medium to high 30 seconds. Add sour cream and milk; beat until combined. Beat in 1½ cups of the shredded cheeses. Stir in artichokes, spinach, green onions, and garlic. Transfer dip to an extra-large oven-going skillet. Sprinkle with remaining ½ cup shredded cheeses.

3. Bake 15 minutes. Remove skillet from oven. Arrange rolls with sides touching on top of hot dip (rolls will fit snugly and cover entire surface). Lightly brush roll tops with melted butter then sprinkle with Parmesan cheese.
5. Bake 15 to 20 minutes or until rolls are golden and dip is hot. Let stand 10 minutes before serving. **MAKES 24 SERVINGS.**
PER SERVING *147 cal., 8 g fat (5 g sat. fat), 24 mg chol., 242 mg sodium, 13 g carb., 1 g fiber, 5 g pro.*

GARLICKY SPINACH AND FETA DIP

PREP 15 minutes

BAKE 20 minutes at 425°F

- 3 cloves garlic, minced
- 1 Tbsp. olive oil
- 10 oz. fresh arugula or spinach
- 8 oz. fresh spinach
- 1 8-oz. pkg. cream cheese, softened
- 1 cup plain Greek yogurt
- 1 cup mayonnaise
- ⅓ cup sliced pitted Kalamata olives
- ¼ tsp. freshly ground black pepper
- 1 cup crumbled feta cheese (4 oz.)
- ½ cup chopped green onions

  Pita chips, multigrain crackers, and/or assorted cut-up vegetables

IF YOU DON'T HAVE A SMALL OVEN-GOING SKILLET, TRANSFER THE DIP TO A SHALLOW OVEN-SAFE DISH BEFORE BAKING.

1. Preheat oven to 425°F. In a 4- to 6-quart Dutch oven cook and stir garlic in hot oil over medium heat 1 minute. Gradually add arugula and spinach; cook and stir until greens wilt. Drain well; cool slightly. Press out any excess liquid from greens. Using kitchen scissors, snip the greens into bite-size pieces.

2. In a bowl combine the greens, the next five ingredients (through pepper), ¾ cup of the feta, and ⅓ cup of the green onions. Transfer dip to a seasoned or generously greased 8- to 9-inch heavy oven-going skillet. Sprinkle with remaining ¼ cup feta cheese.

3. Bake 20 minutes or until heated through and bubbly around the edge. Sprinkle with remaining 2 Tbsp. green onions. Serve dip with chips, crackers, and/or vegetables. **MAKES 32 SERVINGS.**

PER SERVING *86 cal., 8 g fat (3 g sat. fat), 13 mg chol., 114 mg sodium, 1 g carb., 0 g fiber, 2 g pro.*

JALAPEÑO CRAB AND CORN DIP

PREP 30 minutes

BAKE 15 minutes at 425°F

- 2 Tbsp. butter
- 1 cup frozen whole kernel corn
- ½ cup chopped red sweet pepper
- 1 clove garlic, minced
- ½ cup sour cream
- ½ cup mayonnaise
- ½ cup sliced pickled jalapeño chile peppers, drained and chopped
- 1 tsp. Worcestershire sauce
- 1 tsp. hot pepper sauce (optional)
- 2 6- to 6.5-oz. cans crabmeat, drained, flaked, and cartilage removed
- 1 cup shredded Monterey Jack cheese (4 oz.)
- 2 Tbsp. grated Parmesan cheese

    Scoop-shape or lime-flavor tortilla chips

PICKLED JALAPEÑO PEPPERS GIVE THIS CHEESY DIP A TANGY, SPICY KICK. IF YOU WANT A MILDER DIP, SUBSTITUTE PICKLED SWEET PEPPERS OR BANANA PEPPERS.

1. Preheat oven to 425°F. In a generously greased medium oven-going skillet heat butter over medium heat until melted. Add corn, sweet pepper, and garlic; cook 5 minutes or until tender.

2. In a bowl combine sour cream, mayonnaise, jalapeño peppers, Worcestershire sauce, and, if desired, hot pepper sauce. Stir in corn mixture, crabmeat, and Monterey Jack cheese. Transfer to the oven-going skillet.

3. Sprinkle dip with Parmesan cheese. Bake 15 minutes or until golden and bubbly around the edges. Serve with tortilla chips. **MAKES 28 SERVINGS.**

Slow Cooker Directions Prepare as directed through Step 2, using any medium skillet. Heat dip over low heat before transferring to a greased 1½-quart slow cooker. Cover and cook on low 1½ to 2 hours or until bubbly. Sprinkle with Parmesan cheese. Serve with tortilla chips.

PER SERVING *74 cal., 6 g fat (2 g sat. fat), 20 mg chol., 124 mg sodium, 2 g carb., 0 g fiber, 3 g pro.*

BREAKFAST & BRUNCH

DENVER OMELET

4 eggs

⅛ tsp. salt

⅛ tsp. black pepper

2 Tbsp. butter

⅔ cup chopped green sweet pepper

⅔ cup chopped red sweet pepper

¼ cup chopped onion

4 thin slices deli-style cooked ham

½ of an avocado, seeded, peeled, and sliced

2 thin slices deli-style American, provolone, or cheddar cheese

THIS WESTERN-STYLE OMELET IS STUFFED WITH ALL THE CLASSIC FILLINGS—HAM, ONION, AND SWEET PEPPERS—PLUS SLICES OF CREAMY AVOCADO AND CHEESE.

1. In a bowl whisk together eggs, salt, and black pepper.

2. In a large nonstick skillet with flared sides melt 1 Tbsp. of the butter over medium heat. Add sweet peppers and onion; cook 3 minutes or until vegetables are tender, stirring occasionally. Remove vegetables from skillet; keep warm.

3. For each omelet, in the same skillet melt 1½ tsp. of the remaining butter over medium-high heat. Pour about half of the egg mixture into skillet; stir in one-fourth of the vegetables. Cook over medium heat; as egg mixture begins to set, run a spatula around the edge, lifting so uncooked portion flows underneath. Continue cooking until eggs are set but still shiny.

4. Place half of the ham, avocado, and cheese in center of omelet. With a spatula lift and fold an edge of the omelet about one-third of the way toward the center. Fold the opposite edge toward center and transfer to a warm plate; cover to keep warm. Spoon remaining cooked vegetables over omelets before serving. **MAKES 2 SERVINGS.**

PER SERVING *414 cal., 31 g fat (14 g sat. fat), 428 mg chol., 896 mg sodium, 13 g carb., 5 g fiber, 20 g pro.*

SMOKED SALMON EGG WHITE OMELET

3 egg whites, 2 egg whites and 1 whole egg, or ½ cup refrigerated or frozen egg product, thawed

½ tsp. snipped fresh dill

⅛ tsp. salt

Dash bottled hot pepper sauce

½ tsp. olive oil

1 Tbsp. desired-flavor semisoft cheese

¾ oz. thinly sliced smoked salmon (lox-style)

¼ cup broccoli florets, cooked until tender (optional)

Snipped fresh dill

1 Tbsp. sour cream

LOOK FOR LOX-STYLE, COLD-SMOKED SALMON FOR THIS OMELET. ITS FLAVOR IS MILDER THAN HOT-SMOKED SALMON, WHICH COULD OVERPOWER THE OTHER INGREDIENTS.

1. In a bowl whisk together the first four ingredients (through hot pepper sauce).

2. In a medium nonstick skillet with flared sides heat oil over medium-high heat. Pour egg white mixture into skillet. Cook over medium heat without stirring. As mixture begins to set, run a spatula around the edge, lifting egg mixture so uncooked portion flows underneath. Continue cooking until eggs are set but still shiny.

3. Top half the omelet with cheese, salmon, and, if desired, broccoli. Lift and fold the unfilled half of omelet over filling. Slide omelet onto a plate; sprinkle with additional dill and serve with sour cream. **MAKES 1 SERVING.**

PER SERVING *180 cal., 12 g fat (6 g sat. fat), 26 mg chol., 982 mg sodium, 2 g carb., 0 g fiber, 16 g pro.*

ITALIAN BREAKFAST BURRITO

START TO FINISH 25 minutes

2 Tbsp. olive oil

2 cups fresh baby spinach, chopped

1 6-oz. jar marinated artichoke hearts, drained

3 oz. thinly sliced prosciutto, chopped

½ cup lightly packed fresh basil leaves, snipped

⅓ cup finely chopped shallots

2 cloves garlic, minced

8 eggs

Dash salt

Dash black pepper

6 10-inch flour tortillas

½ cup basil pesto

1½ cups shredded mozzarella cheese (6 oz.)

1 15-oz. container refrigerated marinara sauce, heated

THESE UNIQUE BREAKFAST BURRITOS ARE A TASTY FUSION OF MEXICAN AND ITALIAN CUISINES. TANGY MARINATED ARTICHOKE HEARTS AND SAVORY PROSCIUTTO MAKE THEM SPECIAL ENOUGH TO SERVE WHEN YOU HAVE GUESTS.

1. In a large skillet heat oil over medium heat. Add the next six ingredients (through garlic). Cook and stir just until spinach is wilted.

2. In a bowl whisk together eggs, salt, and pepper. Pour over vegetables in skillet. Cook over medium heat, without stirring, until mixture begins to set. With a spatula, lift and fold the partially cooked eggs so the uncooked portion flows underneath. Continue cooking until egg mixture is cooked through but still glossy and moist. Remove from heat.

3. Stack tortillas and wrap in white paper towels. Microwave 30 to 60 seconds or just until warm. Spread tortillas with pesto to within 1 inch of the edges; sprinkle with cheese. Divide egg mixture among tortillas. Fold in opposite sides; roll up tortillas. Serve with warm marinara sauce. **MAKES 6 BURRITOS.**

PER BURRITO *538 cal., 32 g fat (9 g sat. fat), 317 mg chol., 1,371 mg sodium, 35 g carb., 2 g fiber, 27 g pro.*

MEAT-LOVER'S SCRAMBLED EGGS

START TO FINISH 20 minutes

6 eggs
⅓ cup milk or half-and-half
Dash black pepper
4 oz. bulk pork sausage
3 slices bacon, chopped
⅓ cup diced cooked ham
Salsa (optional)

MAKE A SPICED-UP VERSION OF THESE SPECIAL SCRAMBLED EGGS USING HOT ITALIAN-STYLE SAUSAGE OR UNCOOKED CHORIZO (CASINGS REMOVED) IN PLACE OF THE BULK SAUSAGE.

1. In a bowl whisk together eggs, milk, and black pepper.
2. In a large skillet cook sausage and bacon over medium heat until sausage is browned and bacon is crisp. Remove from skillet and drain on paper towels, reserving 1 Tbsp. drippings in skillet. Pat sausage and bacon with paper towels to remove additional fat.

3. Add egg mixture to the reserved drippings in skillet. Cook over medium heat, without stirring, until mixture begins to set. Sprinkle with sausage, bacon, and ham. With a spatula, lift and fold the partially cooked egg mixture so the uncooked portion flows underneath. Continue cooking until egg mixture is cooked through but still glossy and moist. Remove from heat. If desired, serve with salsa. **MAKES 3 SERVINGS.**

PER SERVING *191 cal., 14 g fat (6 g sat. fat), 384 mg chol., 382 mg sodium, 2 g carb., 0 g fiber, 14 g pro.*

BACON-PEA-SWISS SCRAMBLE

START TO FINISH **25 minutes**

Nonstick cooking spray

2 slices turkey bacon, cut crosswise into thin strips

3 eggs

2 Tbsp. reduced-sodium chicken broth

¼ to ½ tsp. sriracha sauce

¼ cup frozen peas, thawed and drained

¼ cup grape or cherry tomatoes, quartered

2 Tbsp. finely shredded Swiss cheese

2 tsp. snipped fresh Italian parsley

TURKEY BACON OR LOWER-SODIUM, LESS-FAT BACON ARE GOOD OPTIONS IN THIS LIGHT AND HEALTHY VEGGIE AND EGG SCRAMBLE. FILL OUT THE MEAL BY SERVING IT WITH WHOLE GRAIN TOAST OR TORTILLAS.

1. Coat a medium nonstick skillet with cooking spray; heat skillet over medium heat. Add bacon; cook 2 minutes or until browned. Remove bacon; discard any fat. Return skillet to medium-low heat.

2. In a bowl whisk together eggs, broth, and sriracha. Stir in bacon and peas.

3. Pour egg mixture into hot skillet. Cook over medium-low heat, without stirring, until mixture begins to set. With a spatula, lift and fold the partially cooked egg mixture so the uncooked portion flows underneath. Continue cooking until almost set. Fold in tomatoes, cheese, and parsley. Cook 30 seconds more or until egg mixture is cooked through but still glossy and moist. **MAKES 2 SERVINGS.**

PER SERVING *194 cal., 12 g fat (5 g sat. fat), 302 mg chol., 372 mg sodium, 5 g carb., 1 g fiber, 15 g pro.*

ASPARAGUS AND PROSCIUTTO FRITTATA

START TO FINISH 25 minutes

8 eggs, lightly beaten

½ cup milk

1 Tbsp. snipped fresh thyme or 1 tsp. dried thyme, crushed

⅛ tsp. black pepper

2 Tbsp. olive oil

6 fresh asparagus spears, trimmed and cut into 1½-inch pieces

1 cup chopped prosciutto

¼ to ½ cup shredded cheddar cheese (1 to 2 oz.)

THIS SIMPLE BUT SPECIAL FRITTATA CAN BE ON YOUR TABLE IN JUST 25 MINUTES, MAKING IT A PERFECT BREAKFAST OPTION FOR BUSY WEEKEND MORNINGS.

1. Preheat broiler. In a bowl whisk together eggs, milk, thyme, and pepper.
2. In a large broiler-proof skillet heat oil over medium heat. Add asparagus; cook and stir 4 minutes or until asparagus is crisp-tender. Stir in prosciutto.
3. Pour egg mixture over asparagus mixture in skillet. Cook over medium heat, without stirring, until mixture begins to set. With a spatula, lift the partially cooked egg mixture so the uncooked portion flows underneath. Continue cooking until eggs are set but still shiny.

4. Place skillet under the broiler, 4 to 5 inches from the heat. Broil 1 to 2 minutes or just until top is set. Sprinkle with cheese. **MAKES 4 SERVINGS.**

PER SERVING *285 cal., 21 g fat (6 g sat. fat), 443 mg chol., 430 mg sodium, 4 g carb., 1 g fiber, 19 g pro.*

FRITTATA WITH TOMATOES

START TO FINISH 25 minutes

- 8 eggs, lightly beaten
- ½ cup milk
- ½ cup chopped thinly sliced prosciutto
- 2 Tbsp. snipped fresh basil
- ¼ tsp. salt
- ⅛ tsp. black pepper
- 2 Tbsp. olive oil
- 2 cups cherry tomatoes
- ½ to 1 cup chopped thawed, frozen artichoke hearts
- ½ cup chopped red onion
- ¼ cup shredded Parmesan cheese (1 oz.)

A LIVELY CHERRY TOMATO-BASIL TOPPING GIVES THIS FRITTATA A UNIQUE TOUCH OF FRESHNESS. NO BASIL ON HAND? SWAP IN ANOTHER FRESH HERB—ITALIAN PARSLEY, THYME, CHIVES, OREGANO, OR DILL WOULD ALSO BE DELICIOUS.

1. Preheat broiler. In a bowl whisk together eggs, milk, prosciutto, 1 Tbsp. of the basil, the salt, and pepper.

2. In a large broiler-proof skillet heat oil over medium heat. Add tomatoes; cook 1 minute, stirring once or twice. Transfer to a bowl. Stir in the remaining 1 Tbsp. basil. In the same skillet cook artichoke hearts and red onion 4 minutes, stirring occasionally.

3. Pour egg mixture over artichoke mixture in skillet. Cook over medium heat, without stirring, until mixture begins to set. With a spatula, lift egg mixture so the uncooked portion flows underneath. Continue cooking until egg mixture is almost set (surface will be moist). Sprinkle with cheese.

4. Place skillet under broiler, 4 to 5 inches from the heat. Broil 1 to 2 minutes or just until top is set. Top with the tomato-basil mixture. **MAKES 4 SERVINGS.**

PER SERVING *443 cal., 21 g fat (6 g sat. fat), 443 mg chol., 563 mg sodium, 4 g carb., 1 g fiber, 19 g pro.*

POTATO FRITTATA

PREP **25 minutes**

BAKE **18 minutes at 375°F**

STAND **5 minutes**

- 2 Tbsp. olive oil
- 1 lb. Yukon gold or russet potatoes, thinly sliced
- 2 large carrots, thinly sliced
- 12 eggs, lightly beaten
- ½ cup chopped green onions
- ¼ tsp. salt
- ¼ tsp. black pepper
- ½ cup yellow cherry tomatoes, halved
- 1 Tbsp. snipped fresh Italian parsley or cilantro
- 1 clove garlic, minced

THIS ITALIAN-STYLE OMELET CAN BE SERVED WARM OR AT ROOM TEMPERATURE. IF YOU DON'T HAVE YELLOW CHERRY TOMATOES, FEEL FREE TO USE ANY VARIETY OF FRESH TOMATOES IN THE TOPPING FOR THE FRITTATA.

1. Preheat oven to 375°F. In a large oven-going nonstick skillet heat oil over medium heat. Add potatoes; cook 5 minutes. Add carrots; cook 5 minutes more or until potatoes and carrots are tender and lightly browned, turning occasionally.

2. In a bowl whisk together eggs, half of the green onions, the salt, and pepper. Pour egg mixture over potatoes. Bake 18 minutes or until frittata appears dry on top. Let stand on a wire rack 5 minutes.

3. Meanwhile, for green onion relish, in a bowl gently toss together the remaining green onions, the cherry tomatoes, parsley, and garlic.

4. Using a narrow spatula, loosen edges of frittata from skillet. Place a large serving platter over skillet. Carefully invert skillet onto platter. Serve with green onion relish. **MAKES 6 SERVINGS.**

PER SERVING *258 cal., 14 g fat (4 g sat. fat), 372 mg chol., 267 mg sodium, 18 g carb., 3 g fiber, 15 g pro.*

SPICY SICILIAN STRATA

PREP 35 minutes

BAKE 45 minutes at 350°F

CHILL 2 hours

STAND 10 minutes

5   cups 1-inch cubes French bread

    Nonstick cooking spray

1   3.5-oz. pkg. sliced pepperoni, coarsely chopped

¼   cup chopped pepperoncini salad peppers, drained

½   of a 10-oz. pkg. frozen chopped spinach, thawed and well drained

¼   cup chopped oil-pack dried tomatoes, drained

1   cup shredded Italian-blend cheeses (4 oz.)

3   eggs, lightly beaten

1½ cups milk

1   tsp. dried Italian seasoning, crushed

¼   tsp. salt

    Dash cayenne pepper

¼   cup grated Parmesan cheese

THIS SAVORY LAYERED BREAD PUDDING FEATURES SPINACH, PEPPERONI, SPICY PEPPERS, AND CHEESE. TOASTING THE BREAD BEFORE BUILDING THE CASSEROLE ALLOWS IT TO SOAK UP MORE OF THE FLAVORFUL EGG MIXTURE.

1. Preheat oven to 350°F. Spread bread cubes in a 15×10-inch baking pan. Bake 10 minutes, stirring once.

2. Coat a large oven-going skillet with cooking spray. Transfer half of the bread cubes to the prepared skillet. Top with half of the pepperoni and pepperoncini peppers, and all of the spinach and dried tomatoes. Sprinkle with ½ cup of the Italian-blend cheeses. Top with the remaining bread cubes, pepperoni, pepperoncini, and Italian cheeses.

3. In a bowl whisk together eggs, milk, Italian seasoning, salt, and cayenne pepper. Slowly pour over layers in skillet; press down lightly with the back of a large spoon. Sprinkle with Parmesan cheese. Cover and chill 2 to 24 hours.

4. Preheat oven to 350°F. Bake, uncovered, 35 to 45 minutes or until a knife inserted near the center comes out clean (170°F). Let stand 10 minutes before serving. **MAKES 6 SERVINGS.**

PER SERVING *316 cal., 18 g fat (8 g sat. fat), 146 mg chol., 1,006 mg sodium, 22 g carb., 2 g fiber, 18 g pro.*

CHEESY HAM CHILAQUILES

PREP 20 minutes

BAKE 15 minutes at 350°F

5 6-inch corn tortillas, cut into 1-inch strips

3 cups salsa

1 cup reduced-sodium chicken broth

½ of a 16-oz. pkg. diced cooked ham (about 1½ cups)

Sliced fresh jalapeño chile peppers* (optional)

1 cup shredded cheddar cheese (4 oz.)

¼ cup sour cream

1 recipe Fried Eggs (optional)

THIS MEXICAN CLASSIC WAS INVENTED AS A WAY TO USE LEFTOVER MEAT AND TORTILLAS. MAKE THIS BREAKFAST-STYLE VERSION WHEN YOU HAVE EXTRA HAM AND TORTILLAS ON HAND.

1. Preheat oven to 350°F. Spread tortilla strips in a single layer on a large baking sheet. Bake 15 minutes or until crisp. Set aside a few tortilla strips.

2. In an extra-large skillet bring salsa to simmering over medium heat; stir in broth. Return to simmering. Simmer, uncovered, 2 minutes. Stir in ham.

3. Stir the remaining tortilla strips into salsa mixture. Simmer, uncovered, 3 minutes or until tortilla strips soften and salsa thickens slightly.

4. Sprinkle with reserved tortilla strips and, if desired, jalapeño peppers. Serve with cheese, sour cream, and, if desired, Fried Eggs. **MAKES 6 SERVINGS.**

*Tip Chile peppers contain oils that can irritate your skin and eyes. Wear plastic or rubber gloves when working with them.

PER SERVING *226 cal., 12 g fat (6 g sat. fat), 46 mg chol., 657 mg sodium, 19 g carb., 1 g fiber, 13 g pro.*

FRIED EGGS In a large skillet melt 2 tsp. butter over medium heat. (Or coat an unheated skillet with cooking spray; heat skillet over medium heat until hot.) Break 4 eggs into skillet. Sprinkle with salt and black pepper. Reduce heat to low; cook eggs 3 to 4 minutes or until whites are completely set and yolks start to thicken. For fried eggs over easy or over hard, when the whites are completely set and the yolks start to thicken, turn eggs and cook 30 seconds more (over easy) or 1 minute more (over hard).

EGG 'N' PROVOLONE BREAKFAST CASSEROLE

PREP 25 minutes

CHILL overnight

BAKE 45 minutes at 325°F

12 oz. bacon, coarsely chopped

¾ cup chopped shallots or onion

2 cloves garlic, minced

6 1-inch slices French bread

2 Tbsp. butter, softened

1 cup shredded provolone or Swiss cheese (4 oz.)

6 eggs

1½ cups half-and-half or whole milk

1 tsp. dry mustard

½ tsp. salt

¼ tsp. black pepper

IF YOU HAVE A LOAF OF FRENCH BREAD THAT'S PAST ITS PEAK, THIS MAKE-AHEAD RECIPE IS PERFECT FOR TRANSFORMING IT INTO AN INDULGENT CASSEROLE.

1. In a large skillet cook bacon over medium heat until crisp. Using a slotted spoon, remove bacon and drain on paper towels, reserving 1 Tbsp. drippings in skillet. Add shallots and garlic to the reserved drippings. Cook and stir until garlic is fragrant and just starting to brown. Remove from heat.

2. Meanwhile, grease a large oven-going skillet or 8-inch square baking dish. Spread one side of the bread slices with butter; cut into 1-inch cubes. Place half of the bread cubes in the prepared skillet. Sprinkle with half of the bacon. Top with the remaining bread cubes and bacon. Spoon shallot mixture over layers in skillet; sprinkle with cheese (skillet will be full).

3. In a bowl whisk together the remaining ingredients. Gradually pour egg mixture over layers in skillet; cover and chill overnight.

4. Preheat oven to 325°F. Bake casserole, uncovered, 45 to 50 minutes or until center is set (170°F). **MAKES 8 SERVINGS.**

PER SERVING *521 cal., 37 g fat (21 g sat. fat), 259 mg chol., 836 mg sodium, 19 g carb., 1 g fiber, 18 g pro.*

HUEVOS TACOS CON QUESO

START TO FINISH **25 minutes**

2 tsp. olive oil

½ cup chopped red onion

2 cloves garlic, minced

1 15-oz. can no-salt-added pinto beans or black beans, drained

½ tsp. ground cumin

¼ tsp. kosher salt

¼ tsp. dried oregano, crushed

⅛ tsp. cayenne pepper

½ cup water

Nonstick cooking spray

10 eggs, lightly beaten

8 6-inch corn tortillas, warmed

½ cup shredded reduced-fat Mexican-style four-cheese blend (2 oz.)

½ cup salsa

Fresh cilantro (optional)

Bottled hot pepper sauce (optional)

TO WARM THE TORTILLAS FOR THESE BREAKFAST TACOS, WRAP THE STACKED TORTILLAS IN PAPER TOWELS AND MICROWAVE 20 TO 40 SECONDS OR UNTIL JUST HEATED THROUGH. OR WRAP THE TORTILLAS IN FOIL AND BAKE THEM IN A 350°F OVEN ABOUT 10 MINUTES.

1. In a large nonstick skillet heat oil over medium heat. Add red onion; cook 4 minutes or until softened, stirring occasionally. Add garlic; cook and stir 30 seconds. Remove from heat. Stir in beans, cumin, salt, oregano, and cayenne pepper, mashing beans with the back of a spoon. Return to heat; stir in the water, continuing to mash beans with the spoon. Simmer, uncovered, until beans thicken and reach spreading consistency (beans won't be completely smooth). Remove mixture from skillet; keep warm.

2. Rinse and dry skillet. Coat skillet with cooking spray; heat over medium heat. Pour eggs into skillet. Cook over medium heat, without stirring, until eggs begin to set. With a spatula, lift and fold the partially cooked eggs so the uncooked portion flows underneath. Continue cooking until eggs are cooked through but still glossy and moist. Remove from heat.

3. Spread mashed beans on warm tortillas; top with cooked eggs. Sprinkle with cheese; fold tortillas in half. Top with salsa. If desired, sprinkle with cilantro and/or serve with hot pepper sauce. **MAKES 4 SERVINGS.**

PER 2 TACOS *402 cal., 19 g fat (6 g sat. fat), 474 mg chol., 605 mg sodium, 31 g carb., 6 g fiber, 26 g pro.*

SAVORY EGG AND SWEET POTATO SCRAMBLE

START TO FINISH 35 minutes

8 eggs

⅓ cup milk

½ tsp. ground cumin

¼ tsp. salt

¼ tsp. black pepper

1 Tbsp. butter

2 medium sweet potatoes (about 1 lb.), peeled, quartered lengthwise, and thinly sliced

2 Tbsp. sliced green onion

2 cups fresh baby spinach

Snipped fresh Italian parsley

Bottled hot pepper sauce (optional)

FOR THE BEST FLAVOR AND PRESENTATION, USE ORANGE-FLESH SWEET POTATOES FOR THIS BREAKFAST SCRAMBLE. WHEN BUYING SWEET POTATOES, LOOK FOR ONES THAT ARE FIRM FROM END TO END AND HAVE SMOOTH, UNBLEMISHED SKINS.

1. In a bowl whisk together eggs, milk, cumin, salt, and pepper.

2. In a large skillet melt butter over medium heat. Add sweet potatoes and green onion. Cook 8 minutes or just until potatoes are tender and lightly browned, stirring occasionally. Add spinach. Cook and stir 1 minute or until slightly wilted.

3. Pour egg mixture over potato mixture in skillet. Cook over medium heat, without stirring, until egg mixture begins to set. With a spatula, lift and fold the partially cooked egg mixture so the uncooked portion flows underneath. Continue cooking 2 to 3 minutes or until egg mixture is cooked through but still glossy and moist. Remove from heat. Sprinkle with parsley. If desired, serve with hot pepper sauce. **MAKES 4 SERVINGS.**

PER SERVING *258 cal., 13 g fat (5 g sat. fat), 381 mg chol., 390 mg sodium, 20 g carb., 3 g fiber, 15 g pro.*

SPANISH EGGS

START TO FINISH 35 minutes

1 Tbsp. olive oil

½ cup chopped onion

1 small fresh Anaheim chile pepper, seeded and chopped (tip, page 51)

1 clove garlic, minced

4 large tomatoes, chopped

1 small zucchini, halved lengthwise and thinly sliced

1 tsp. dried savory or cilantro, crushed

½ tsp. salt

4 eggs

Crumbled queso fresco

Snipped fresh cilantro

Corn tortillas, warmed (optional)

ANAHEIM CHILES ARE SWEET WITH JUST A LITTLE BITE. IF YOU CAN'T FIND THIS CHILE VARIETY, SUBSTITUTE A SEEDED JALAPEÑO OR A POBLANO PEPPER.

1. In a large skillet heat oil over medium heat. Add onion, Anaheim pepper, and garlic; cook 5 minutes or until tender, stirring occasionally. Add tomatoes, zucchini, savory, and salt; cook 5 minutes more or until tomatoes release their liquid and zucchini is tender, stirring occasionally.

2. Break an egg into a cup and slip egg into the tomato mixture. Repeat with the remaining three eggs, allowing each egg an equal amount of space in the tomato mixture. Simmer, covered, 3 to 5 minutes or until egg whites are completely set and yolks begin to thicken but are not hard. Remove from heat.

3. Sprinkle with queso fresco and cilantro. If desired, serve with corn tortillas. **MAKES 4 SERVINGS.**

PER SERVING *176 cal., 10 g fat (3 g sat. fat), 191 mg chol., 395 mg sodium, 13 g carb., 3 g fiber, 11 g pro.*

HASH BROWNS O'BRIEN

PREP 25 minutes

COOK 25 minutes

1¼ lb. russet potatoes

¼ tsp. salt

⅛ tsp. black pepper

1 to 2 Tbsp. olive oil

1 Tbsp. butter

½ cup chopped red onion

½ cup chopped red sweet pepper

½ cup chopped green sweet pepper

2 cloves garlic, minced

1 Tbsp. snipped fresh sage

FOR PERFECTLY BROWNED, CRISPY HASH BROWNS, MAKE SURE TO REMOVE ALL MOISTURE FROM THE SHREDDED POTATOES BEFORE THEY GO INTO THE SKILLET. IF YOU DON'T HAVE A SALAD SPINNER, DRY THE POTATOES BY PATTING THEM DRY WITH PAPER TOWELS.

1. Peel and coarsely shred potatoes. Place potatoes in a large bowl; add enough water to cover potatoes. Stir well. Drain in a colander set in the sink. Repeat rinsing and draining two or three times until water runs clear. Drain again, pressing out as much water as you can with a rubber spatula. Line a salad spinner with paper towels; add potatoes and spin (see tip, above). Repeat, if necessary, until potatoes are dry. Return potatoes to the large bowl. Sprinkle with salt and black pepper; toss gently to combine.

2. In a large nonstick skillet heat 1 Tbsp. of the oil and the butter over medium heat until butter foams. Add onion, sweet peppers, and garlic; cook 5 minutes or until tender, stirring occasionally.

3. Stir in potatoes and sage; spread into an even layer. Gently press with the back of a spatula to form a cake. Cook, without stirring, 12 minutes or until bottom is golden brown and crisp.

4. Invert a plate over skillet. Carefully transfer potatoes to plate. If necessary, add the remaining 1 Tbsp. oil to skillet. Slide potatoes back into skillet, uncooked side down. Cook 8 to 12 minutes more or until bottom is golden brown. **MAKES 6 SERVINGS.**

SPICY HASH BROWNS O'BRIEN: Prepare as directed, except substitute ¼ cup chopped fresh Anaheim or poblano chile pepper (tip, page 51) for the green sweet pepper.

PER SERVING *123 cal., 4 g fat (2 g sat. fat), 5 mg chol., 121 mg sodium, 20 g carb., 2 g fiber, 2 g pro.*

SWEET DUTCH BABY

PREP 10 minutes

BAKE 35 minutes at 425°F

3 Tbsp. granulated sugar

¾ tsp. ground cinnamon

1 cup thinly sliced Braeburn apple

2 Tbsp. butter, cut up

3 eggs, room temperature

½ cup milk, room temperature

½ cup all-purpose flour

½ tsp. vanilla

⅛ tsp. salt

Powdered sugar

FOR OPTIMAL PUFFINESS IN THIS BAKED PANCAKE, USE A HEAVY SKILLET AND BE SURE TO KEEP THE OVEN DOOR CLOSED WHILE IT'S BAKING. TOP THE PANCAKE WITH YOUR FAVORITE JAMS, SYRUP, HONEY, OR A SIMPLE DUSTING OF POWDERED SUGAR.

1. Preheat oven to 425°F. In a bowl stir together 2 Tbsp. of the granulated sugar and ¼ tsp. of the cinnamon. Add apple slices; toss gently to coat.

2. Place butter in a large oven-going skillet. Place skillet in oven 2 minutes or until butter is melted. Remove from oven; swirl skillet to coat surface. Spread apple slices evenly in skillet. Bake 10 minutes or until apples are slightly softened and butter is bubbling and beginning to brown around the edges.

3. Meanwhile, in a blender combine eggs, milk, flour, vanilla, salt, remaining 1 Tbsp. granulated sugar, and remaining ½ tsp. cinnamon. Cover and blend 1 minute or until well mixed and frothy.

4. Pour batter over apples. Bake 25 to 30 minutes or until puffed and golden brown. Cool slightly in skillet on a wire rack (pancake will deflate). Lightly sprinkle warm pancake with powdered sugar. **MAKES 6 SERVINGS.**

PER SERVING *160 cal., 7 g fat (3 g sat. fat), 105 mg chol., 128 mg sodium, 20 g carb., 1 g fiber, 5 g pro.*

PUFFED OVEN PANCAKE WITH BROWN SUGAR-BANANA SAUCE

PREP 15 minutes

BAKE 20 minutes at 400°F

2   Tbsp. butter, cut up

4   eggs, lightly beaten

⅔   cup all-purpose flour

⅔   cup fat-free milk

¼   tsp. salt

½   cup butter

⅓   cup packed brown sugar

3   medium bananas, sliced

2   Tbsp. light rum or apple juice

    Powdered sugar (optional)

    Whipped cream (optional)

ALSO CALLED A GERMAN BAKED PANCAKE, THIS MORNING TREAT PUFFS IN THE PAN THEN FALLS INTO ITS SIGNATURE CONCAVE SHAPE AFTER IT'S DONE BAKING, PROVIDING THE PERFECT PLACE FOR THE SWEET BANANA SAUCE.

1. Preheat oven to 400°F. Place the 2 Tbsp. butter in an extra-large oven-going skillet. Place skillet in oven 3 to 5 minutes or until butter is melted. Remove from heat; swirl skillet to coat surface.

2. Meanwhile, in a bowl combine eggs, flour, milk, and salt; whisk until smooth. Pour batter into the hot skillet. Bake 20 to 25 minutes or until puffed and well browned.

3. For sauce, in a small saucepan cook and stir the ½ cup butter and the brown sugar over medium heat until melted. Add bananas; cook 2 minutes or until heated through, stirring gently. Carefully stir in rum; heat through.

4. Spoon sauce over warm pancake. If desired, lightly sprinkle with powdered sugar. Cut into wedges and, if desired, serve with whipped cream. **MAKES 8 SERVINGS.**

PER SERVING *290 cal., 17 g fat (10 g sat. fat), 144 mg chol., 222 mg sodium, 28 g carb., 1 g fiber, 6 g pro.*

4 WAYS WITH PANCAKES

START TO FINISH 25 minutes

1¾ cups all-purpose flour

2 Tbsp. granulated sugar

1 Tbsp. baking powder

¼ tsp. salt

1 egg, lightly beaten

1½ cups milk

3 Tbsp. vegetable oil

Butter (optional)

Desired syrup (optional)

EVERYONE LOVES BASIC PANCAKES, BUT YOU CAN SHAKE THINGS UP A BIT BY TRYING ONE OF THESE FOUR DELICIOUS CREATIVE VARIATIONS.

1. In a large bowl stir together flour, granulated sugar, baking powder, and salt. In a bowl combine egg, milk, and oil. Add egg mixture all at once to flour mixture. Stir just until moistened (batter should be slightly lumpy).

2. For standard-size pancakes, pour about ¼ cup batter onto a hot, lightly greased griddle or heavy skillet. Spread batter, if necessary. For dollar-size pancakes, use about 1 Tbsp. batter. Cook over medium heat 1 to 2 minutes on each side or until pancakes are golden brown. Turn over when surfaces are bubbly and edges are slightly dry. Serve warm with butter and syrup, if desired. **MAKES 12 SERVINGS.**

PER SERVING *126 cal., 5 g fat (1 g sat. fat), 18 mg chol., 191 mg sodium, 18 g carb., 0 g fiber, 3 g pro.*

BERRY-CORNMEAL PANCAKES Prepare as directed, except use 1¼ cups all-purpose flour and add ½ cup cornmeal. Stir ½ cup fresh raspberries into batter. Top pancakes with butter, additional raspberries and/or strawberries, and raspberry or strawberry syrup.

PER SERVING *223 cal., 9 g fat (3 g sat. fat), 28 mg chol., 233 mg sodium, 34 g carb., 2 g fiber, 4 g pro.*

PUMPKIN-CRANBERRY PANCAKES Prepare as directed, except increase all-purpose flour to 2 cups, substitute packed brown sugar for

the granulated sugar, and use 2 eggs. Stir ½ cup canned pumpkin, ¼ cup dried cranberries, and 1½ tsp. pumpkin pie spice into batter. Top pancakes with whipped cream, caramel-flavor ice cream topping, additional dried cranberries, and chopped pecans.

PER SERVING *240 cal., 8 g fat (3 g sat. fat), 44 mg chol., 233 mg sodium, 38 g carb., 1 g fiber, 4 g pro.*

APPLE-BACON PANCAKES Prepare as directed, except substitute whole wheat flour for the all-purpose flour and packed brown sugar for the granulated sugar. Stir ½ cup chopped apples, ¼ cup crumbled cooked bacon, and 1 tsp. ground cinnamon into batter. Top pancakes with sautéed apple slices, crumbled cooked bacon, and maple syrup.

PER SERVING *239 cal., 9 g fat (2 g sat. fat), 30 mg chol., 377 mg sodium, 33 g carb., 2 g fiber, 8 g pro.*

CHOCOLATE-BANANA PANCAKES Prepare as directed, except stir ½ cup sliced banana and ⅓ cup miniature semisweet chocolate pieces into batter. Top with additional sliced banana and chocolate-flavor syrup.

PER SERVING *227 cal., 6 g fat (2 g sat. fat), 18 mg chol., 205 mg sodium, 38 g carb., 2 g fiber, 4 g pro.*

MANGO-BANANA COCONUT CREPES WITH CAJETA SYRUP

PREP 25 minutes

COOK 25 minutes

- 2 eggs, lightly beaten
- 2 cups coconut milk
- 1 Tbsp. butter, melted
- 1 Tbsp. vanilla
- 6 Tbsp. sugar
  - Dash salt
- 2 cups all-purpose flour
  - Butter
- 1 cup heavy cream
- ¼ tsp. ground cinnamon
- 2 cups chopped fresh or refrigerated mangoes
- 2 cups thinly sliced bananas
- 1 recipe Cajeta Syrup
  - Toasted shredded coconut (tip, page 15) (optional)

CAJETA—A SPECIALTY MEXICAN INGREDIENT—IS A THICK, CARAMELIZED SYRUP MADE FROM GOAT MILK. IF YOU CAN'T FIND IT, SUBSTITUTE CANNED DULCE DE LECHE OR CARAMEL ICE CREAM TOPPING.

1. In a bowl whisk together the first four ingredients (through vanilla). Whisk in ¼ cup of the sugar and the salt. Add flour, whisking until smooth. If desired, cover and chill up to 24 hours before using.

2. In a large skillet heat an additional 1 tsp. butter over medium-high heat until melted. Pour in ¼ cup of the batter; lift and tilt skillet to spread batter evenly. Cook 1 minute or until edges and bottom are lightly browned. Gently run a rubber spatula around the edges to loosen; carefully flip crepe over and cook about 30 seconds or until bottom is lightly browned. Transfer to a warm platter. Repeat with remaining batter to make 14 crepes total.

3. In a chilled bowl beat heavy cream, cinnamon, and remaining 2 Tbsp. sugar with a mixer on medium until soft peaks form (tips curl).

4. For each filled crepe, place one of the crepes on a work surface. Spoon 2 Tbsp. of the whipped cream onto half of crepe; top with about 2 Tbsp. of the mangoes and about 2 Tbsp. of the bananas. Fold unfilled half of crepe over filling; fold in half again. Drizzle crepes with Cajeta Syrup and, if desired, sprinkle with toasted coconut. **MAKES 7 SERVINGS.**

CAJETA SYRUP In a bowl stir together 6 Tbsp. cajeta and 6 Tbsp. maple syrup. Makes ¾ cup.

To Make Ahead Cool crepes completely and stack on an oven-going plate. Cover tightly with plastic wrap and chill 2 to 24 hours. To serve, preheat oven to 300°F. Remove plastic wrap. Bake crepes 15 minutes or until warm.

PER SERVING *637 cal., 31 g fat (21 g sat. fat), 119 mg chol., 149 mg sodium, 80 g carb., 3 g fiber, 9 g pro.*

SANDWICHES & PIZZAS

HAM AND GRAPE GRILLED CHEESE

START TO FINISH **20 minutes**

1½ cups seedless red grapes, coarsely chopped

8 slices marble rye bread or sourdough bread

12 oz. shaved ham

1 cup shredded Jarlsberg or Swiss cheese (or 4 oz. sliced)

Butter or olive oil

YOU'LL LOVE THE SWEET-SAVORY COMBINATION OF SUCCULENT GRAPES AND SALT-CURED HAM. JARLSBERG CHEESE—A NORWEGIAN SPECIALTY—ADDS A BUTTERY, NUTTY FLAVOR TO THE SANDWICH. IF YOU CAN'T FIND IT, SWISS CHEESE MAKES A GREAT SUBSTITUTE.

1. In a large nonstick skillet cook grapes over medium heat 2 to 4 minutes or just until grapes are softened. Drain off any liquid.

2. Layer four of the bread slices with ham, grapes, and cheese. Top with remaining four bread slices. Lightly spread outside of sandwiches with butter or brush with olive oil.

3. Rinse and dry the skillet. Preheat skillet over medium heat. Place sandwiches, half at a time if necessary, in skillet. Cook 2 to 3 minutes or until bread is toasted. Turn sandwiches and cook 1 to 2 minutes more or until bread is toasted and filling is heated through. **MAKES 4 SANDWICHES.**

PER SANDWICH *534 cal., 26 g fat (14 g sat. fat), 97 mg chol., 1,495 mg sodium, 48 g carb., 4 g fiber, 28 g pro.*

CAPRESE-STYLE GRILLED CHEESE EGG SANDWICHES

START TO FINISH 30 minutes

4 eggs

¼ cup water

¼ tsp. salt

⅛ tsp. black pepper

2 Tbsp. butter

4 large slices country-style whole grain or white bread

8 slices mozzarella cheese

6 large fresh basil leaves

6 slices tomato

1 Tbsp. olive oil

YOU CAN CHOOSE FRESH OR REGULAR MOZZARELLA FOR THESE SANDWICHES. IF YOU USE FRESH MOZZARELLA, POP IT IN THE FREEZER FOR ABOUT 10 MINUTES TO MAKE IT EASIER TO SLICE.

1. In a bowl combine eggs, the water, salt, and pepper. Beat with a fork until combined but not frothy. For each omelet, in a small nonstick skillet with flared sides melt 1 Tbsp. of the butter over medium-high heat. Pour half the egg mixture into skillet. Cook over medium heat. As mixture sets, run a spatula around edges of skillet, lifting egg mixture so the uncooked portion flows underneath. Continue cooking and lifting edges until egg mixture is set but is still shiny. Lift and fold one edge of the omelet to the opposite edge. Slide omelet onto a warm plate. Cover to keep warm.

2. Layer two of the bread slices with half of the cheese, basil, tomato, omelets, and remaining cheese; top with remaining two bread slices. If necessary, secure sandwiches with wooden toothpicks.

3. In a large skillet heat oil over medium-high heat. Add sandwiches; cook 4 to 5 minutes or until bread is toasted and cheese is melted, turning once. Cut sandwiches in half. **MAKES 4 SANDWICHES.**

PER ½ SANDWICH *420 cal., 28 g fat (13 g sat. fat), 246 mg chol., 770 mg sodium, 18 g carb., 3 g fiber, 24 g pro.*

FARMERS MARKET GRILLED CHEESE

START TO FINISH 30 minutes

2 cups fresh baby spinach

¼ cup mayonnaise

2 cloves garlic, minced

¼ tsp. salt

¼ tsp. black pepper

8 ½-inch-thick slices sourdough bread

2 Tbsp. olive oil

½ of a 3.5-oz. pkg. garlic-and-herb goat cheese (chèvre), softened

1 small zucchini, thinly sliced lengthwise

1 medium tomato, sliced

A SPECIAL MAYO-BASED SPREAD MADE WITH FRESH SPINACH AND GARLIC ADDS A CREATIVE SPIN TO TRADITIONAL GRILLED CHEESE. FOR A PEPPERY BITE, USE FRESH BABY ARUGULA FOR THE SPINACH.

1. In a blender or food processor combine 1 cup of the spinach, the mayonnaise, garlic, salt, and pepper. Cover and blend or process until smooth.

2. Brush one side of each bread slice with oil; place bread, oiled sides down, on waxed paper. Spread four of the bread slices with cheese; layer with zucchini, tomato, and remaining 1 cup spinach. Spread the remaining four bread slices with some of the mayonnaise mixture; set aside remaining mixture for serving. Place bread slices, spread sides down, on vegetables.

3. In an extra-large skillet cook sandwiches over medium-high heat 6 to 8 minutes or until bread is toasted, turning once. Pass the reserved mayonnaise mixture. **MAKES 4 SANDWICHES.**

PER SANDWICH *369 cal., 22 g fat (6 g sat. fat), 15 mg chol., 636 mg sodium, 32 g carb., 3 g fiber, 10 g pro.*

MUENSTER, CABBAGE, AND APPLE SANDWICHES

START TO FINISH **35 minutes**

- 1 medium onion, halved lengthwise and thinly sliced
- ¼ cup cider vinegar
- ¼ cup water
- 1 cup coarsely shredded cabbage
- 1 large cooking apple, such as Granny Smith, Rome Beauty, or Jonathan, thinly sliced
- 1 Tbsp. stone-ground mustard
- 1 cup shredded Muenster cheese (4 oz.)
- 8 slices caraway rye bread

  Nonstick cooking spray

CHOOSE A FIRM, TART APPLE, SUCH AS GRANNY SMITH OR JONATHAN, TO USE FOR THE FILLING IN THESE SANDWICHES. THESE VARIETIES WILL HOLD THEIR SHAPE WHEN COOKED AND WON'T BREAK DOWN AND CREATE A MUSHY FILLING.

1. In a medium skillet combine onion, vinegar, and the water. Bring just to boiling; reduce heat. Simmer, covered, 3 minutes. Stir in cabbage; simmer, covered, 3 minutes. Stir in apple slices. Simmer, covered, 3 minutes more or just until vegetables and apple are tender; drain. Stir in mustard.

2. Layer cabbage mixture and cheese on four of the bread slices. Top with the remaining four bread slices. Lightly coat outside of sandwiches with cooking spray.

3. Preheat a large nonstick skillet over medium heat. Place sandwiches, half at a time if necessary, in skillet. Weight down with a heavy skillet and cook 1 to 2 minutes or until bread is toasted. Turn sandwiches, weight down, and cook 1 to 2 minutes more or until bread is toasted and filling is heated through. **MAKES 4 SANDWICHES.**

PER SANDWICH *296 cal., 11 g fat (6 g sat. fat), 27 mg chol., 606 mg sodium, 39 g carb., 5 g fiber, 12 g pro.*

TARRAGON TUNA MELTS

START TO FINISH 30 minutes

⅓ cup mayonnaise

3 Tbsp. snipped fresh Italian parsley

2 Tbsp. snipped fresh chives

1 to 2 Tbsp. snipped fresh tarragon or 2 tsp. dried tarragon, crushed

1 tsp. finely shredded lemon peel

2 tsp. lemon juice

1 tsp. Dijon-style mustard

⅛ tsp. black pepper

1 12-oz. can solid white tuna (water pack), drained and flaked

8 ½-inch slices sourdough bread

8 to 12 thin tomato slices (optional)

1 cup shredded sharp white cheddar cheese (4 oz.)

2 Tbsp. butter, softened

THE DISTINCTIVE LICORICE-LIKE FLAVOR OF TARRAGON, PLUS OTHER HERBS, GIVES THE TUNA SALAD IN THESE MELTS A FRESH KICK. SOURDOUGH BREAD ADDS A HINT OF TANGINESS. IF YOU PREFER, YOU CAN USE ITALIAN OR FRENCH BREAD INSTEAD.

1. In a bowl combine the first eight ingredients (through pepper). Stir in tuna, breaking up any large pieces with a fork.

2. Spread four of the bread slices with tuna mixture; top with tomato slices, if desired, and cheese. Place the remaining four bread slices on top of cheese. Spread the outside of sandwiches with butter.

3. Place sandwiches on a large nonstick griddle over medium heat. (Or cook sandwiches, half at a time, in a large nonstick skillet.) Cook 6 to 8 minutes or until cheese is melted and bread is golden, turning once. **MAKES 4 SANDWICHES.**

PER SANDWICH *550 cal., 34 g fat (12 g sat. fat), 95 mg chol., 988 mg sodium, 27 g carb., 2 g fiber, 32 g pro.*

SPANISH GRILLED SANDWICHES

PREP **30 minutes**

CHILL **2 hours**

COOK **8 minutes per batch**

- 1 6-oz. jar marinated artichoke hearts, undrained
- 1 7-oz. jar roasted red sweet peppers, drained and cut into strips (about 1 cup)
- ⅔ cup jalapeño-stuffed green olives, sliced
- 1 medium onion, thinly sliced and separated into rings
- 1 Tbsp. snipped fresh Italian parsley
- 1 small clove garlic, minced
- ⅛ tsp. dried oregano, crushed
- ⅛ tsp. ground cumin
- 2 8-inch Italian flatbreads (focaccia), split in half horizontally, or 4 sandwich rolls, such as pan cubano, bolillos, or hoagie buns, split
- 1 lb. thinly sliced roast beef or pork
- 8 oz. sliced provolone cheese
- 4 tsp. olive oil

FOCACCIA BREAD IS SOLD WITH A VARIETY OF FLAVORFUL TOPPINGS. POPULAR OPTIONS INCLUDE ROASTED GARLIC, DRIED TOMATO, AND OLIVE. CHOOSE YOUR FAVORITE FOR THESE MEDITERRANEAN-INSPIRED HOT SANDWICHES.

1. For relish, drain artichokes, reserving marinade. Thinly slice artichokes. In a medium bowl combine sliced artichokes, the reserved marinade, and the next seven ingredients (through cumin). Cover and chill 2 to 24 hours, tossing occasionally.

2. To assemble sandwiches, spoon relish onto bottom halves of focaccia. Top with meat and cheese; replace top halves of focaccia.

3. In an extra-large skillet heat 2 tsp. of the oil over medium heat. Add two of the sandwiches; weight down with a large heavy skillet. Cook 4 to 5 minutes or until bread is toasted. Turn sandwiches over, weight down, and cook 4 to 5 minutes or until bread is toasted and cheese melts. Remove from skillet and keep warm while cooking remaining sandwiches. Cut sandwiches in half. **MAKES 4 SANDWICHES.**

PER SANDWICH *834 cal., 32 g fat (13 g sat. fat), 118 mg chol., 1,588 mg sodium, 76 g carb., 4 g fiber, 60 g pro.*

SKILLET PANINI 4 WAYS

START TO FINISH 25 minutes

Filling

8   slices French, sourdough, or Italian bread, sliced ¾ inch thick

2   Tbsp. olive oil or butter, softened

CHOOSE FROM FOUR TASTY FILLINGS FOR THESE SKILLET PANINI, THEN COOK THEM ON YOUR STOVE TOP FOR AN EASY DINNER— NO PANINI PRESS NEEDED.

1. Preheat a large heavy skillet over medium heat. Layer Filling ingredients on four slices of bread. Top with remaining bread slices. Brush outsides of sandwiches with olive oil or spread with butter.

2. Place sandwiches (half at a time, if necessary) in skillet. Weight down sandwiches using another skillet or pan and cook 2 to 3 minutes or until bread is toasted. Turn sandwiches over, weight down, and cook until bread is toasted and cheese melts. **MAKES 4 SANDWICHES.**

ITALIAN BEEF FILLING 1 lb. sliced roast beef; 1 cup drained pickled mixed vegetables (giardiniera), coarsely chopped; 4 slices provolone cheese; and ¼ cup grated Parmesan cheese.
PER SANDWICH *499 cal., 23 g fat (9 g sat. fat), 104 mg chol., 1,434 mg sodium, 32 g carb., 1 g fiber, 43 g pro.*

VEGGIE FILLING 1 cup thinly sliced cucumber, 1 cup fresh spinach, 1 cup drained sliced roasted red sweet peppers, ¼ cup thinly sliced red onion, 4 slices Co-Jack cheese, and ¼ cup ranch dressing.
PER SANDWICH *399 cal., 23 g fat (7 g sat. fat), 29 mg chol., 854 mg sodium, 35 g carb., 2 g fiber, 13 g pro.*

HAM AND APPLE FILLING 12 oz. thinly sliced cooked ham, 8 oz. sliced Brie cheese, 1 cup sliced apple, and 2 Tbsp. Dijon-style mustard.
PER SANDWICH *556 cal., 31 g fat (14 g sat. fat), 105 mg chol., 1,843 mg sodium, 37 g carb., 3 g fiber, 32 g pro.*

CHICKEN-BACON FILLING 12 oz. shredded chicken or turkey (plain or smoked), 8 slices crisp-cooked bacon, 1 cup corn relish, and 4 slices cheddar cheese.
PER SANDWICH *632 cal., 25 g fat (9 g sat. fat), 122 mg chol., 1,099 mg sodium, 55 g carb., 1 g fiber, 45 g pro.*

SMOKED GOUDA AND APRICOT MELTS

START TO FINISH **25 minutes**

½   cup dried apricots, snipped

    Boiling water

⅓   cup sliced, slivered, or chopped almonds, toasted (tip, page 15)

¼   cup thinly sliced green onions

8   slices marbled rye or hearty whole grain bread

2   Tbsp. apricot preserves

4   oz. thinly sliced cooked ham

1   cup shredded smoked Gouda cheese (4 oz.)

¼   to ½ tsp. freshly ground black pepper

    Nonstick cooking spray

GOUDA IS ONE OF THE OLDEST RECORDED CHEESES STILL BEING PRODUCED TODAY. THE FLAVOR OF SMOKED GOUDA PAIRS WELL WITH THE SWEET-TART DRIED APRICOTS.

1. In a bowl combine dried apricots and enough boiling water to cover. Let stand 5 minutes; drain. Stir almonds and green onions into drained apricots.

2. Spread four of the bread slices with apricot preserves. Top with ham. Top with the apricot mixture and cheese; sprinkle with pepper. Add the remaining four bread slices. Lightly coat outsides of sandwiches with cooking spray.

3. Preheat a large nonstick skillet over medium heat. Place sandwiches, half at a time if necessary, in skillet. Weight down with another skillet and cook 1 to 2 minutes or until bread is toasted. Turn sandwiches, weight down, and cook 1 to 2 minutes more or until bread is toasted and filling is heated through. **MAKES 4 SANDWICHES.**

PER SANDWICH *419 cal., 14 g fat (6 g sat. fat), 48 mg chol., 863 mg sodium, 55 g carb., 5 g fiber, 20 g pro.*

ONE-PAN CHICKEN FLATBREADS

START TO FINISH 35 minutes

½ cup roasted garlic hummus

½ cup plain Greek yogurt

12 oz. skinless, boneless chicken breast halves

4 tsp. lemon-pepper seasoning

1 Tbsp. olive oil

4 7-inch flatbread rounds

½ cup halved grape tomatoes

½ cup sliced English cucumber

¼ cup chopped onion

¼ cup crumbled feta cheese (1 oz.)

Snipped fresh Italian parsley (optional)

Lemon wedges (optional)

TO ENSURE AN EVEN THICKNESS WHEN FLATTENING THE CHICKEN FOR THESE SANDWICHES, USE THE FLAT SIDE OF THE MEAT MALLET TO LIGHTLY POUND THE CHICKEN, WORKING FROM THE CENTER OF THE BREAST OUTWARD.

1. In a bowl combine hummus and the ½ cup yogurt. Place each chicken breast half between two pieces of plastic wrap. Using the flat side of a meat mallet, pound chicken lightly until about ¼ inch thick. Discard plastic wrap. Sprinkle chicken with lemon-pepper seasoning.

2. In an extra-large skillet heat oil over medium-high heat. Add chicken (half at a time if necessary). Cook 4 to 6 minutes or until chicken is no longer pink, turning once. Transfer to a cutting board; let stand 2 minutes. Cut chicken into strips. Carefully wipe skillet dry.

3. Add flatbreads to the same skillet. Cook over medium-high heat 2 to 4 minutes or until toasted, turning once.

4. Top flatbreads with chicken, tomatoes, cucumber, onion, and cheese. If desired, sprinkle with parsley. Serve with hummus mixture and, if desired, additional yogurt and/or lemon wedges. **MAKES 4 SANDWICHES.**

PER SANDWICH *517 cal., 23 g fat (6 g sat. fat), 66 mg chol., 925 mg sodium, 45 g carb., 5 g fiber, 32 g pro.*

SWEET SKILLET MEATBALL BANH MI

START TO FINISH **40 minutes**

- 1 egg, lightly beaten
- ¼ cup fine dry bread crumbs
- 3 Tbsp. soy sauce
- 1 clove garlic, minced
- 1 lb. ground beef
- 3 medium carrots, cut into thin bite-size strips
- 1 medium onion, thinly sliced
- 2 Tbsp. packed brown sugar
- 1 9-oz. pkg. fresh spinach
- 6 hoagie buns, split and toasted

   Fresh Italian parsley leaves (optional)

NO HOAGIE BUNS ON HAND FOR THESE SANDWICHES? YOU CAN SERVE THE MEATBALL–AND–VEGGIE FILLING IN PITA BREAD OR HALVED BAGUETTES. FOR A LOW-CARB OPTION, SPOON THE FILLING INTO LETTUCE LEAVES.

1. In a bowl combine egg, bread crumbs, 1 Tbsp. of the soy sauce, and the garlic. Add ground beef; mix well. Shape into about thirty 1¼-inch meatballs.

2. In an extra-large heavy skillet arrange meatballs in a single layer. Cook over medium-high heat 8 to 10 minutes or until browned on all sides, turning once. Remove from skillet; keep warm.

3. Add carrots and onion to skillet. Cook and stir 3 to 5 minutes or until tender.

4. Return meatballs to skillet. Add brown sugar and remaining 2 Tbsp. soy sauce. Cook 2 minutes more or until meatballs and vegetables are well coated. Add spinach; cook 3 minutes or just until wilted. Serve in hoagie buns. If desired, sprinkle with parsley. **MAKES 6 SANDWICHES.**

PER SANDWICH *445 cal., 15 g fat (5 g sat. fat), 82 mg chol., 1,066 mg sodium, 55 g carb., 4 g fiber, 24 g pro.*

CHILI-CHEESE HOAGIES

PREP 25 minutes

COOK 15 minutes

1   lb. lean ground beef

1   cup chopped onion

1   cup chopped green sweet pepper

2   cloves garlic, minced

1   14.5-oz. can diced tomatoes with chili spices, undrained

¼   tsp. black pepper

8   hoagie buns or French-style rolls, split

8   oz. sliced or shredded Monterey Jack cheese

8   oz. sliced or shredded cheddar cheese

BY REMOVING THE EXCESS BREAD FROM THE INSIDE OF THE HOAGIE BUN, YOU CREATE MORE SPACE FOR THE CHEESES AND CHILI-STYLE FILLING.

1. In a large skillet cook ground beef, onion, sweet pepper, and garlic over medium-high heat until meat is browned and vegetables are tender. Drain off fat.

2. Stir in tomatoes and black pepper. Bring to boiling; reduce heat. Simmer, uncovered, 15 minutes or until mixture is thickened, stirring occasionally.

3. Place buns on a parchment-lined baking pan. Fill buns with chili, Monterey Jack cheese, and cheddar cheese. Broil about 1 minute or just until cheese is melted. **MAKES 8 SANDWICHES.**

PER SANDWICH *738 cal., 31 g fat (15 g sat. fat), 91 mg chol., 1,274 mg sodium, 79 g carb., 5 g fiber, 36 g pro.*

PORK TENDERLOIN SANDWICHES

START TO FINISH 25 minutes

- 1 lb. pork tenderloin
- ¼ cup all-purpose flour
- ¼ tsp. garlic salt
- ¼ tsp. black pepper
- 1 egg, lightly beaten
- 1 Tbsp. milk
- ½ cup seasoned fine dry bread crumbs
- 2 Tbsp. vegetable oil
- 4 large hamburger buns or kaiser rolls, split and toasted

  Ketchup, mustard, tomato slices, onion slices, and/or dill pickle slices

AFTER BEING POUNDED AND BREADED, THE TENDERLOIN PIECES WILL BE TOO LARGE TO FIT INSIDE THE SKILLET ALL AT ONCE. COOK ONE OR TWO AT A TIME, AND KEEP THE COOKED TENDERLOINS WARM ON A BAKING PAN IN A 300°F OVEN UNTIL ALL FOUR ARE COOKED.

1. Trim fat from pork. Cut meat crosswise into four slices. Place each slice between two pieces of plastic wrap. Using the flat side of a meat mallet, pound pork lightly until about ¼ inch thick. Discard plastic wrap.

2. In a shallow dish stir together flour, garlic salt, and pepper. In another shallow dish combine egg and milk. Place bread crumbs in a third shallow dish. Dip tenderloin into flour mixture to coat. Dip into egg mixture, then into bread crumbs, turning to coat.

3. In a large heavy skillet heat oil over medium heat. Cook tenderloins in batches 6 to 8 minutes or until slightly pink in center, turning once.

4. Serve tenderloins in buns with ketchup, mustard, tomato, onion, and/or dill pickles.

MAKES 4 SANDWICHES.

PER SANDWICH *424 cal., 13 g fat (3 g sat. fat), 127 mg chol., 776 mg sodium, 42 g carb., 2 g fiber, 33 g pro.*

STEAKHOUSE BURGERS

PREP **25 minutes**

COOK **35 minutes**

1   Tbsp. butter

1   large sweet onion, thinly sliced (2 cups)

1½ lb. ground beef

2   Tbsp. steak sauce

1¼ tsp. Montreal steak seasoning, divided

1   Tbsp. vegetable oil

4   ¾-oz. slices Swiss cheese (3 oz.)

2   Tbsp. mayonnaise

1   tsp. chopped fresh Italian parsley

4   hamburger buns, split and toasted

1   cup baby arugula

THE KEY TO THE MOST FLAVORFUL AND JUICY BURGERS IS TO USE A GRIND OF ABOUT 85% CHUCK AND 15% SIRLOIN. THIS COMBO WILL HAVE AN IDEAL BEEF-TO-FAT RATIO. LOOK FOR IT IN THE MEAT CASE, ASK YOUR BUTCHER TO GRIND IT FOR YOU, OR GRIND YOUR OWN BURGER BLEND.

1. In a large heavy skillet melt butter over medium-low heat. Add onion. Cook, covered, 13 to 15 minutes or until onion is tender, stirring occasionally. Uncover; cook and stir over medium-high heat 3 to 5 minutes more or until golden. Remove caramelized onion from skillet; cover to keep warm. Wipe skillet.

2. In a bowl combine ground beef, steak sauce, and 1 tsp. of the Montreal steak seasoning; mix well. Shape mixture into four ¾-inch-thick patties. Make a shallow indentation in the center of each patty with your thumb.

3. In the same skillet heat oil over medium heat; add patties. Cook 12 to 15 minutes or until done (160°F), turning once. Top patties with cheese; cover and cook 1 minute more.

4. Meanwhile, in a bowl combine mayonnaise, parsley, and the remaining ¼ tsp. Montreal steak seasoning. Spread cut sides of buns with mayonnaise mixture. Serve patties in buns with caramelized onions and arugula. **MAKES 4 BURGERS.**

PER BURGER *776 cal., 53 g fat (20 g sat. fat), 151 mg chol., 779 mg sodium, 32 g carb., 2 g fiber, 40 g pro.*

GREEK BURGERS

PREP 25 minutes

COOK 16 minutes

1   Tbsp. snipped fresh
    oregano or 1 tsp. dried
    oregano, crushed

2   tsp. Worcestershire sauce

½   tsp. kosher salt

¼   tsp. freshly ground black
    pepper

1½ lb. ground beef sirloin

2   Tbsp. olive oil

1½ cups thickly sliced
    fresh button or cremini
    mushrooms

1   cup red sweet pepper
    strips

2   small red onions, sliced

4   kaiser rolls, split and
    toasted

⅓   cup crumbled feta cheese

NEXT TIME YOU'RE CRAVING BURGERS TAKE THEM BEYOND THE
BASICS BY ENHANCING THEM WITH GREEK-INSPIRED FLAVORS.
USING A HEAVY CAST-IRON SKILLET TO COOK THE BURGERS
GUARANTEES A CRISP, CARAMELIZED, DEEP BROWN CRUST.

1. In a bowl combine half of the fresh or dried
oregano, the Worcestershire sauce, salt, and
black pepper. Add ground beef; mix well. Shape
meat mixture into four ½-inch-thick patties.
2. In a large heavy skillet heat 1 Tbsp. of the oil
over medium-high heat. Add mushrooms, sweet
pepper, and onions; cook 4 to 5 minutes or until
crisp-tender, stirring occasionally. Remove
from heat. Stir in remaining fresh or dried
oregano. Remove vegetables from skillet; cover
to keep warm.

3. Add the remaining 1 Tbsp. oil to skillet; heat
over medium-high heat. Add patties. Cook 12 to
15 minutes or until a thermometer registers
160°F, turning once. (Reduce heat if patties
brown too quickly.)
4. Fill toasted rolls with patties, vegetables, and
cheese. **MAKES 4 BURGERS.**

PER BURGER *652 cal., 37 g fat (13 g sat. fat),
126 mg chol., 840 mg sodium, 37 g carb., 3 g fiber,
41 g pro.*

BUFFALO CHICKEN BURGERS

PREP 20 minutes

COOK 12 minutes

1½ lb. ground chicken or turkey

3 Tbsp. Buffalo wing sauce

1 Tbsp. vegetable oil

1 Tbsp. butter, melted

¼ cup sour cream

2 Tbsp. mayonnaise

3 Tbsp. crumbled blue cheese

1 Tbsp. sliced green onion

4 ciabatta buns or hamburger buns, split and toasted

Green leaf lettuce leaves

Sliced tomato

ENJOY THE FLAVORS OF CLASSIC BUFFALO WINGS IN A FUN-TO-EAT BURGER. GROUND CHICKEN AND TURKEY ARE AVAILABLE, AS A COMBINATION OF WHITE AND DARK MEAT, OR ONLY BREAST MEAT, WHICH IS VERY LEAN. BOTH ARE OFTEN STICKY, SO USE WET HANDS TO SHAPE THE MEAT INTO PATTIES.

1. In a bowl combine ground chicken and 2 Tbsp. of the Buffalo wing sauce; mix well. Shape mixture into four ¾-inch-thick patties.

2. Heat oil in an extra-large nonstick skillet over medium heat. Add patties to hot pan. Cook 12 to 15 minutes or until done (165°F), turning once.

3. In a bowl combine melted butter and the remaining 1 Tbsp. Buffalo wing sauce. Spoon butter mixture on both sides of patties, turning to coat in sauce in skillet.

4. Meanwhile, for blue cheese dressing, in a bowl combine sour cream, mayonnaise, blue cheese, and green onion.

5. Serve patties in buns with additional sauce, lettuce, tomato, and blue cheese dressing.

MAKES 4 BURGERS.

PER BURGER *492 cal., 29 g fat (9 g sat. fat), 166 mg chol., 1037 mg sodium, 24 g carb., 5 g fiber, 34 g pro.*

LENTIL VEGGIE BURGERS

PREP 40 minutes

COOK 10 minutes

¾ cup dry lentils

1¾ cups water

Nonstick cooking spray

8 oz. fresh cremini mushrooms, trimmed and chopped (3 cups)

1 cup peeled and chopped sweet potato

4 cloves garlic, minced

1 cup lightly packed arugula

2 Tbsp. reduced-sodium soy sauce

2 Tbsp. yellow cornmeal

2 Tbsp. olive oil

4 naan or whole-grain pita rounds

Toppings such red pepper jelly and/or sautéed sliced sweet miniature peppers

TO SAVE TIME, SKIP STEP 1 AND USE 2 CUPS PURCHASED COOKED REFRIGERATED LENTILS INSTEAD OF COOKING THEM YOURSELF.

1. In a medium saucepan combine lentils and the water. Bring to boiling; reduce heat. Simmer, covered, 30 minutes or until very soft. Drain any excess water.

2. Meanwhile, coat a very large nonstick skillet with cooking spray. Cook mushrooms, sweet potato, and garlic in skillet over medium heat 6 to 8 minutes or until sweet potato is tender, stirring frequently. Remove from heat; cool slightly. In a food processor combine the sweet potato mixture, 1 cup of the lentils, the arugula, and soy sauce. Cover and process until mixture is nearly smooth. Stir into the remaining cooked lentils until combined (mixture will be soft).

3. Shape lentil mixture into eight ½-inch-thick patties and sprinkle both sides with cornmeal. In the same skillet heat oil over medium heat. Add patties to skillet and cook 10 minutes or until a thermometer registers 165°F, turning once.

4. Meanwhile, warm naan according to package directions. Cut naan in half; top one half with additional arugula, two patties, and desired toppings. **MAKES 8 BURGERS.**

PER 2 BURGERS *521 cal., 13 g fat (2 g sat. fat), 724 mg sodium, 83 g carb., 8 g fiber, 21 g pro.*

SAUSAGE AND SPINACH SKILLET PIZZA

PREP **35 minutes**

BAKE **15 minutes at 475°F**

STAND **7 minutes**

- 1 15-oz. can tomato sauce
- 3 Tbsp. grated Parmesan cheese
- 2 Tbsp. tomato paste
- ¾ tsp. dried oregano, crushed
- ½ tsp. dried basil, crushed
- ⅛ tsp. crushed red pepper
- 1 5- to 6-oz. pkg. fresh baby spinach
- 2 tsp. water
  Olive oil
- 1 lb. frozen pizza or bread dough, thawed
- 8 oz. bulk Italian sausage, cooked and drained
- 1½ to 2 cups shredded mozzarella cheese (6 to 8 oz.)
  Crushed red pepper (optional)

COOKING THE SKILLET PIZZA ON THE STOVE TOP FOR A FEW MINUTES BEFORE BAKING IT GIVES THE CRUST A CRISPY, BROWNED BOTTOM.

1. Preheat oven to 475°F. In a bowl combine tomato sauce, 2 Tbsp. of the Parmesan cheese, the tomato paste, oregano, basil, and the ⅛ tsp. crushed red pepper.

2. Place spinach in a large bowl; sprinkle with the water. Cover with a plate. Microwave 30 seconds. Continue cooking in 10-second intervals just until spinach is wilted. Let stand 2 minutes; carefully remove plate. Transfer spinach to a sieve; press out excess liquid.

3. Brush an extra-large heavy oven-going skillet with oil. On a lightly floured surface, roll pizza dough into a 14-inch circle. Transfer to the prepared skillet. Roll edges to form a rim. Brush dough lightly with oil. Spread tomato sauce mixture over dough; top with sausage and spinach. Sprinkle with mozzarella cheese and the remaining 1 Tbsp. Parmesan cheese.

4. Cook pizza in skillet over medium-high heat 3 minutes. Place skillet in oven. Bake 15 to 20 minutes or until crust and cheeses are lightly browned. Let stand 5 minutes before serving. Using a spatula, slide pizza out of skillet. Cut into wedges. If desired, sprinkle with additional crushed red pepper. **MAKES 6 WEDGES.**

PER WEDGE *449 cal., 23 g fat (9 g sat. fat), 53 mg chol., 1,237 mg sodium, 40 g carb., 3 g fiber, 19 g pro.*

LOADED CHEESEBURGER SKILLET PIZZA

PREP 30 minutes

BAKE 15 minutes at 425°F

1   lb. lean ground beef

¼   tsp. salt

¼   tsp. black pepper

1   Tbsp. vegetable oil

1   lb. purchased prepared fresh or frozen pizza or bread dough, thawed

⅓   cup ketchup

2   Tbsp. yellow mustard

1   cup shredded cheddar cheese (4 oz.)

½   cup shredded mozzarella cheese (2 oz.)

½   cup chopped onion

½   cup dill pickle slices

4   slices bacon, crisp-cooked and crumbled

PREMADE PIZZA DOUGH SAVES A LOT OF TIME WHEN MAKING PIZZA AT HOME. LOOK FOR FRESH DOUGH AT A LOCAL BAKERY, PIZZA PLACE, OR SPECIALTY GROCERY STORE. IF FRESH DOUGH ISN'T AVAILABLE, YOU CAN USE FROZEN BREAD DOUGH FROM YOUR SUPERMARKET'S FREEZER SECTION. THAW THE DOUGH ACCORDING TO PACKAGE DIRECTIONS.

1. Preheat oven to 425°F. In a large skillet cook ground beef until browned, breaking the meat into small pieces as it cooks. Drain off fat. Stir in salt and pepper.

2. Brush an extra-large heavy oven-going skillet with oil. On a lightly floured surface, roll pizza dough into a 14-inch circle. Transfer to prepared skillet, rolling edges to form a rim. Spread ketchup and mustard evenly over the dough. Top with ground beef mixture. Sprinkle with half of each of the cheeses. Top with onion, pickles, and bacon. Sprinkle with the remaining cheeses.

3. Cook pizza in skillet over medium heat 3 minutes. Place skillet in oven. Bake 15 minutes or until crust and cheeses are lightly browned. **MAKES 6 WEDGES.**

PER WEDGE *488 cal., 22 g fat (8 g sat. fat), 80 mg chol., 1,002 mg sodium, 41 g carb., 2 g fiber, 31 g pro.*

DEEP DISH-SKILLET SAUSAGE-PORTOBELLO PIZZA

PREP 45 minutes

RISE 1 hour 15 minutes

BAKE 40 minutes at 400°F

STAND 20 minutes

Olive oil

Cornmeal

1 cup warm water (105°F to 115°F)

1 pkg. active dry yeast

3 to 3½ cups all-purpose flour

⅓ cup olive oil

½ tsp. salt

8 oz. bulk Italian sausage

½ cup chopped onion

4 oz. fresh portobello mushrooms, coarsely chopped

1 14.5-oz. can diced tomatoes, drained

1 tsp. dried oregano, crushed

2 Tbsp. snipped fresh basil

6 oz. shredded part-skim mozzarella cheese

¼ cup grated Parmesan cheese

IF YOU PREFER A MILDER MUSHROOM FLAVOR, YOU CAN USE BABY PORTOBELLO MUSHROOMS—ALSO CALLED CREMINI MUSHROOMS—OR WHITE BUTTON MUSHROOMS IN PLACE OF THE LARGE PORTOBELLO MUSHROOMS IN THE FILLING.

1. Generously grease a large heavy oven-going skillet with olive oil. Sprinkle bottom with cornmeal.

2. In a large mixing bowl combine the warm water and yeast, stirring to dissolve yeast. Let stand 5 minutes. Stir in 1½ cups of the flour, the ⅓ cup oil, and salt. Beat on low 30 seconds. Beat on high 2 minutes. Stir in as much of the remaining flour as you can.

3. Turn dough out onto a lightly floured surface. Knead in enough flour to make a moderately stiff dough that is smooth and elastic. Shape dough into a ball. Place in a lightly greased bowl, turning once to grease surface of dough. Cover and let rise until double in size (50 to 60 minutes). Punch down dough. Let rest 5 minutes.

4. Place dough in prepared skillet. Press and spread dough evenly over bottom and about 1½ inches up the sides of the skillet. Cover and let rise 25 minutes.

5. Meanwhile, preheat oven to 400°F. For filling, in a large skillet cook sausage over medium-high heat until browned; drain off fat. Add onion. Cook over medium-high heat, stirring occasionally, 3 minutes or until onion is just softened. Add mushrooms. Cook 5 minutes more or until mushrooms are softened and liquid has evaporated. Stir in drained tomatoes and oregano. Cook 1 to 2 minutes or until heated through. Stir in basil.

6. Spread mozzarella cheese over dough in skillet. Spoon filling over cheese. Sprinkle with grated Parmesan.

7. Cook pizza in skillet over medium-high heat 3 minutes. Transfer pizza to oven. Bake 40 to 45 minutes or until edges are golden and filling is heated through. Let stand at least 10 minutes before serving. **MAKES 8 WEDGES.**

PER WEDGE *453 cal., 24 g fat (7 g sat. fat), 37 mg chol., 665 mg sodium, 42 g carb., 3 g fiber, 16 g pro.*

EASY BBQ CHICKEN-PINEAPPLE PIZZA

PREP 15 minutes
BAKE 20 minutes at 400°F
STAND 5 minutes

BE SURE TO REMOVE ALL EXCESS JUICE FROM THE PINEAPPLE TO ENSURE IT DOESN'T MAKE THE PIZZA WATERY IN THE CENTER WHEN IT BAKES.

Nonstick cooking spray

1 13.8-oz. pkg. refrigerated pizza dough

½ cup bottled barbecue sauce

1½ cups shredded or chopped purchased roasted chicken or leftover cooked chicken

1½ cups shredded pizza cheese

1 8-oz. can pineapple tidbits, well-drained

¼ cup sliced green onions

2 Tbsp. grated Asiago cheese

1. Preheat oven to 400°F. Lightly coat an extra-large heavy oven-going skillet with nonstick cooking spray. Unroll pizza dough into the skillet. Press dough into bottom and halfway up the sides of the skillet. Bake 5 minutes.

2. Spread barbecue sauce over crust to edges. Top with chicken. Sprinkle with pizza cheese. Top with pineapple tidbits. Bake 15 minutes or until crust is golden. Sprinkle with green onions and Asiago cheese. Let stand 5 minutes before serving. **MAKES 8 WEDGES.**

PER WEDGE *280 cal., 9 g fat (4 g sat. fat), 46 mg chol., 803 mg sodium, 33 g carb., 1 g fiber, 16 g pro.*

BEEF, PORK & LAMB

STEAK WITH PAN SAUCE

PREP 20 minutes

STAND 30 minutes

ROAST 10 minutes at 400°F

2 beef top loin or ribeye steaks, cut 1 to 1½ inches thick, or 4 beef tenderloin steaks, cut 1 to 1½ inches thick (1½ to 2 lb. total)

½ tsp. kosher salt

½ tsp. freshly ground black pepper

6 Tbsp. cold unsalted butter

½ cup dry red wine or apple juice

⅓ cup reduced-sodium beef broth

3 Tbsp. finely chopped shallot or 2 cloves garlic, minced

2 Tbsp. heavy cream (no substitutes)

SEARING STEAKS BEFORE ROASTING THEM IN THE SKILLET CREATES A CRISP, CARAMELIZED EXTERIOR AS WELL AS FLAVORFUL BROWNED BITS ON THE SKILLET THAT BECOME THE FOUNDATION FOR A RICH PAN SAUCE.

1. Allow steaks to stand at room temperature 30 minutes. Preheat oven to 400°F. Trim fat from steaks. Pat steaks dry with paper towels. Sprinkle salt and pepper over both sides of steaks. Heat a large oven-going skillet over medium-high heat. Add 2 Tbsp. butter to hot skillet; reduce heat to medium. Add steaks; cook 4 minutes or until browned, turning once. Transfer skillet to oven. Roast, uncovered, 10 to 13 minutes or until medium rare (145°F). Transfer steaks to a serving platter; keep warm.

2. For pan sauce, drain fat from skillet. Add wine, broth, and shallot to skillet. Bring to boiling, whisking constantly to scrape up any crusty browned bits from skillet. Boil gently, uncovered, over medium heat 6 minutes or until liquid is reduced to about ¼ cup.

3. Whisk in heavy cream. Boil gently 1 to 2 minutes more or until slightly thickened. Whisk in the remaining 4 Tbsp. butter, 1 Tbsp. at a time, until butter is melted and sauce is thickened. Serve steaks with pan sauce. **MAKES 4 SERVINGS.**

Tip Vary the flavor of the sauce with one of these stir-ins: 1 tsp. snipped fresh thyme, tarragon, or oregano with the shallot; 1 tsp. Dijon-style mustard or balsamic vinegar with the shallot; or 1 tsp. rinsed and drained capers into the finished sauce

PER SERVING *529 cal., 39 g fat (19 g sat. fat), 173 mg chol., 437 mg sodium, 3 g carb., 37 g pro.*

ESPRESSO-RUBBED STEAK WITH GREEN CHILE PESTO

START TO FINISH **30 minutes**

1 1½-lb. beef flank steak

2 tsp. chili powder

1 tsp. kosher salt or sea salt

1 tsp. instant espresso coffee powder

½ tsp. garlic powder

½ tsp. dried oregano, crushed

½ tsp. black pepper

1 Tbsp. extra-virgin olive oil

1 recipe Green Chile Pesto

Fresh cilantro leaves (optional)

SCORING FLANK STEAK BEFORE APPLYING THE RUB ALLOWS THE SEASONINGS TO PENETRATE DEEPLY INTO THE MEAT.

1. Trim fat from steak. Score both sides of steak in a diamond pattern by making shallow diagonal cuts at 1-inch intervals. In a bowl combine the next six ingredients (through black pepper.) Sprinkle mixture over both sides of steak; rub in with your fingers.

2. Coat an extra-large nonstick skillet with the oil; heat skillet over medium-high heat. Add steak; reduce heat to medium. Cook 12 to 14 minutes for medium rare (145°F) or 14 to 16 minutes for medium (160°F), turning once.

3. Thinly slice steak diagonally across the grain. Serve with Green Chile Pesto. If desired, sprinkle with cilantro. **MAKES 8 SERVINGS.**

GREEN CHILE PESTO Cut 2 medium Anaheim or poblano chile peppers in half lengthwise; remove stems, seeds, and membrane (tip, page 51). Coarsely chop peppers. In a food processor combine the chopped peppers, ½ cup fresh cilantro leaves, ¼ cup crumbled Cotija cheese, 2 Tbsp. pine nuts, 2 cloves garlic, and ¼ tsp. crushed red pepper. Cover and process until finely chopped. Season with salt and black pepper. With processor running, add ⅓ cup olive oil in a steady stream through feed tube to form a coarse paste.

PER SERVING *244 cal., 17 g fat (3 g sat. fat), 31 mg chol., 335 mg sodium, 4 g carb., 1 g fiber, 20 g pro.*

GREEK FLAT IRON STEAKS

START TO FINISH 25 minutes

1 lemon

2 6- to 8-oz. boneless beef shoulder top blade (flat iron) steaks

Salt

Black pepper

1 tsp. dried rosemary, crushed

4 tsp. olive oil

2 cups grape tomatoes, halved, if desired

2 cloves garlic, minced

⅓ cup pitted green olives, halved

¼ cup crumbled feta cheese (1 oz.)

FLAT-IRON STEAKS—ALSO CALLED TOP BLADE STEAKS OR TOP BONELESS CHUCK STEAKS—ARE AN ECONOMICAL BUT FLAVORFUL CUT FROM THE BEEF CHUCK SECTION.

1. Remove 1 tsp. zest from lemon. Cut the lemon into wedges. Trim fat from steaks. Cut each steak in half and generously sprinkle both sides with salt, pepper, and rosemary. Rub in with your fingers.

2. In a large nonstick skillet heat 2 tsp. of the oil over medium-high heat. Add steaks; cook 8 to 10 minutes or until medium rare (145°F), turning once. Remove from skillet; keep warm.

3. Add remaining 2 tsp. oil to skillet. Add tomatoes and garlic; cook over medium-high heat 3 minutes or until tomatoes start to soften and burst. Remove from heat. Stir in olives and reserved lemon zest.

4. Serve steaks with tomato mixture. Sprinkle with cheese and serve with reserved lemon wedges. **MAKES 4 SERVINGS.**

PER SERVING *220 cal., 13 g fat (4 g sat. fat), 56 mg chol., 467 mg sodium, 6 g carb., 2 g fiber, 20 g pro.*

QUICK PAPRIKA STEAKS WITH TOMATO GRAVY

START TO FINISH **30 minutes**

- ¼ cup all-purpose flour
- 1 tsp. paprika
- ¾ tsp. salt
- ¾ tsp. black pepper
- 4 4-oz. beef breakfast or skillet steaks, about ½ inch thick
- 3 Tbsp. olive oil
- 2 oz. queso fresco or Monterey Jack cheese, thinly sliced
- 6 medium tomatoes, seeded and cut up
- 6 cloves garlic, minced
- 1 to 2 Tbsp. snipped fresh sage

  Arugula (optional)

BREAKFAST STEAKS ARE REFERRED TO BY VARIOUS TERMS—SKILLET STEAKS, WAFER STEAKS, OR SANDWICH STEAKS, JUST TO NAME A FEW. IN GENERAL, THIS TYPE OF STEAK IS SMALL, THIN, AND RELATIVELY INEXPENSIVE.

1. In a shallow dish stir together flour, paprika, ½ tsp. of the salt, and ¼ tsp. of the pepper. Dip steaks into flour mixture, turning to coat (reserve any remaining flour mixture). In an extra-large skillet heat 1 Tbsp. of the oil over medium-high heat. Reduce heat to medium. Cook steaks in hot oil 8 to 10 minutes for medium (160°F), turning once and topping with cheese the last 2 minutes. Remove steaks from skillet; keep warm.

2. Meanwhile, place tomatoes in a food processor. Cover and process with on-off pulses until tomatoes are coarsely chopped.

3. For tomato gravy, in the same skillet heat the remaining 2 Tbsp. oil over medium heat. Add garlic; cook and stir 1 minute or until golden. Stir in tomatoes, sage, remaining ¼ tsp. salt and ½ tsp. pepper, and any remaining flour mixture. Bring to boiling; reduce heat. Simmer, uncovered, 5 minutes or until gravy reaches desired consistency.

4. Divide arugula among plates, if desired, and top with steaks. Spoon some tomato gravy over steaks; pass remaining gravy. **MAKES 4 SERVINGS.**

PER SERVING *365 cal., 21 g fat (6 g sat. fat), 77 mg chol., 615 mg sodium, 16 g carb., 3 g fiber, 29 g pro.*

STEAK WITH SPICY BALSAMIC GLAZE

PREP 15 minutes

STAND 20 minutes

COOK 15 minutes

1 lb. boneless beef top sirloin steak, about 1-inch thick, trimmed of fat

½ cup water

½ cup apple cider

¼ cup Worcestershire sauce

¼ cup balsamic vinegar

¼ tsp. crushed red pepper

Nonstick cooking spray

Salt

Black pepper

¼ cup honey

A QUICK SOAK IN MARINADE INFUSES THE STEAK WITH THE TANGY-SWEET FLAVORS OF APPLE CIDER AND BALSAMIC VINEGAR. THE MARINADE THEN SIMMERS AWAY, TURNING INTO A RICH HONEY GLAZE.

1. Place steak in a resealable plastic bag. Add the next five ingredients (through crushed red pepper). Seal bag, turning to coat meat. Let stand 20 minutes, turning occasionally.

2. Heat a large skillet coated with cooking spray over medium heat. Remove beef from marinade, reserving marinade. Season beef with salt and black pepper. Cook 8 to 12 minutes for medium rare (145°F) or 12 to 15 minutes for medium (160°F), turning once. Remove steak from skillet; keep warm.

3. Add marinade and honey to skillet; whisk to combine. Bring to boiling; boil gently, uncovered, 7 minutes or until reduced to ⅓ cup. Serve glaze with steak. **MAKES 4 SERVINGS.**

PER SERVING *286 cal., 5 g fat (2 g sat. fat), 68 mg chol., 384 mg sodium, 34 g carb., 1 g fiber, 26 g pro.*

SKILLET PORK CHOPS WITH BUTTER BEANS, PEAS, AND CHARRED GREEN ONIONS

PREP 25 minutes

ROAST 8 minutes at 400°F

4 pork loin rib chops, cut 1¼ inches thick

1 lemon

2 Tbsp. snipped fresh Italian parsley

2 Tbsp. snipped fresh tarragon

¼ tsp. salt

¼ tsp. black pepper

1 Tbsp. olive oil

6 green onions, cut into 2-inch pieces

1 15.5- to 16-oz. can butter beans, rinsed and drained

1 5-oz. pkg. fresh baby spinach

1 cup shelled fresh English peas or frozen peas, thawed

1 lemon, cut into wedges (optional)

AS THE PORK CHOPS ROAST WITH THE GREEN ONIONS, THE EDGES OF THE ONIONS BECOME DEEPLY CARAMELIZED AND INTENSELY FLAVORED.

1. Preheat oven to 400°F. Trim fat from chops. Remove 2 tsp. zest and 1 Tbsp. juice from lemon. In a bowl combine lemon zest, parsley, tarragon, salt, and pepper. Sprinkle over chops; rub in with your fingers.

2. In an extra-large oven-going skillet heat oil over medium-high heat. Add chops to skillet; cook 6 minutes or until browned, turning once. Stir green onions into skillet around chops. Transfer skillet to the oven. Roast 8 to 10 minutes or until a thermometer registers 145°F. Remove chops from skillet; keep warm.

3. Stir beans, spinach, peas, and lemon juice into green onions in skillet. Cook and stir until beans are heated through and peas are tender. If desired, serve with lemon wedges. **MAKES 4 SERVINGS.**

PER SERVING *467 cal., 22 g fat (5 g sat. fat), 99 mg chol., 603 mg sodium, 27 g carb., 8 g fiber, 43 g pro.*

SPICY SKILLET PORK CHOPS

PREP **35 minutes**

COOK **10 minutes**

STAND **5 minutes**

- 3 cups frozen whole kernel corn
- 2 10-oz. cans diced tomatoes and green chiles, undrained
- 4 cloves garlic, minced
- 1 tsp. ground cumin
- ½ tsp. bottled hot pepper sauce
- 8 boneless pork loin chops, cut ¾ inch thick
- 1 tsp. chili powder
- 1 Tbsp. vegetable oil
- 2 medium onions, cut into thin wedges
  Hot cooked rice
  Fresh cilantro (optional)

YOU CAN MAKE THIS SKILLET AHEAD AND KEEP IT IN THE FREEZER FOR A QUICK DINNER. JUST COOK THE RECIPE THROUGH STEP 3, TRANSFER IT TO A FREEZER BAG OR CONTAINER, AND FREEZE FOR UP TO 3 MONTHS. THAW IT IN THE REFRIGERATOR ONE DAY BEFORE YOU NEED IT, AND REHEAT IT IN A COVERED SKILLET OVER MEDIUM-LOW HEAT AT DINNERTIME.

1. In a bowl combine the first five ingredients (through hot pepper sauce).

2. Trim fat from chops; sprinkle both sides with chili powder. In an extra-large skillet heat oil over medium-high heat. Add chops; cook 4 minutes or until browned, turning once. Remove chops, reserving drippings in skillet.

3. Add onions to the reserved drippings; cook and stir over medium heat 3 minutes. Stir in corn mixture; top with chops. Bring to boiling; reduce heat. Simmer, covered, 10 to 12 minutes or until a thermometer registers 145°F. Remove chops from skillet; cover and let stand 5 minutes before serving.

4. Sprinkle hot cooked rice with cilantro, if desired. **MAKES 8 SERVINGS.**

PER SERVING *396 cal., 10 g fat (2 g sat. fat), 107 mg chol., 369 mg sodium, 32 g carb., 2 g fiber, 42 g pro.*

BREADED PORK WITH CABBAGE AND KALE

START TO FINISH 20 minutes

1¼ lb. boneless center-cut pork loin roast

2 cups corn bread stuffing mix, crushed

2 Tbsp. olive oil

2 cups sliced red cabbage

6 cups coarsely chopped fresh kale

⅓ cup balsamic vinegar

Salt

Black pepper

USING A PURCHASED CORN BREAD STUFFING MIX FOR THE BREADING GIVES THIS PAN-FRIED PORK A LOT OF FLAVOR USING JUST ONE INGREDIENT.

1. Trim fat from meat. Cut meat into four slices. Place each meat slice between two pieces of plastic wrap. Using the flat side of a meat mallet, pound meat lightly until about ¼ inch thick. Remove plastic wrap. Place stuffing mix in a shallow dish; add meat, turning to coat.

2. In an extra-large skillet heat 1 Tbsp. of the oil over medium-high heat. Add two of the meat slices; cook 4 to 6 minutes or until coating is golden brown and meat is slightly pink in the center, turning once. Remove from skillet; keep warm. Repeat with the remaining oil and meat slices.

3. Wipe skillet with a paper towel; add cabbage. Cook and stir until cabbage is crisp-tender. Add kale and vinegar; cook and stir just until wilted. Sprinkle lightly with salt and pepper. **MAKES 4 SERVINGS.**

PER SERVING *394 cal., 14 g fat (2 g sat. fat), 78 mg chol., 769 mg sodium, 35 g carb., 4 g fiber, 32 g pro.*

GARLIC PORK AND SWEET POTATO HASH

START TO FINISH **30 minutes**

3   small sweet potatoes,
    scrubbed and chopped
    (4 cups)

1½ lb. pork tenderloin

2   Tbsp. reduced-sodium soy
    sauce

    Black pepper

3   Tbsp. vegetable oil

8   cloves garlic, thinly sliced

¼   cup sliced green onion

2   Tbsp. honey

2   Tbsp. water

BE SURE TO COOK THE SLICED GARLIC JUST UNTIL IT'S GOLDEN BUT NOT TOO BROWNED. IF GARLIC GETS OVERLY BROWNED, IT CAN TAKE ON A BITTER FLAVOR.

1. Place sweet potatoes in a bowl; cover with vented plastic wrap. Microwave 8 minutes, stirring once. Carefully remove plastic wrap.

2. Meanwhile, trim fat from meat; cut into 1-inch slices. To butterfly slices, make a horizontal cut three-fourths of the way through each slice; open and flatten slightly. Brush slices with 1 Tbsp. of the soy sauce and sprinkle lightly with pepper.

3. In an extra-large skillet heat oil over medium-high heat. Add garlic; cook and stir just until it begins to turn golden. Remove from skillet. Add meat to hot skillet. Cook 4 to 6 minutes or until a thermometer registers 145°F, turning once. Remove from skillet; keep warm.

4. For hash, transfer sweet potatoes to hot skillet. Cook until potatoes begin to crisp, stirring occasionally. Add green onion; cook and stir 1 minute.

5. For sauce, in the hot skillet whisk together honey, the water, and remaining 1 Tbsp. soy sauce. Cook and stir until bubbly. Top hash with meat and garlic, and drizzle with sauce. **MAKES 4 SERVINGS.**

PER SERVING *451 cal., 16 g fat (3 g sat. fat), 107 mg chol., 449 mg sodium, 39 g carb., 4 g fiber, 37 g pro.*

MEDITERRANEAN LAMB SKILLET

START TO FINISH 25 minutes

- ½ cup dried orzo
- 8 lamb rib chops, cut 1 inch thick

  Salt

  Black pepper
- 2 tsp. olive oil
- 3 cloves garlic, minced
- 1 14.5-oz. can diced tomatoes with basil, garlic, and oregano, undrained
- 1 Tbsp. balsamic vinegar
- 2 tsp. snipped fresh rosemary
- ⅓ cup halved, pitted Kalamata olives

SERVE THIS EASY-TO-MAKE DINNER WHEN YOU NEED A QUICK BUT SPECIAL MEAL. NO ONE WILL EVER KNOW IT ONLY TOOK 25 MINUTES TO PREPARE.

1. Cook orzo according to package directions; drain and keep warm. Meanwhile, trim fat from chops. Sprinkle chops with salt and pepper. In a large skillet heat olive oil over medium heat. Add chops; cook 9 to 11 minutes for medium (160°F), turning once. Remove chops from skillet; keep warm.

2. Stir garlic into drippings in skillet. Cook and stir 1 minute. Stir in tomatoes, vinegar, and rosemary. Bring to boiling; reduce heat. Simmer, uncovered, 5 minutes. Stir in orzo and olives. Return chops to skillet; heat through.

MAKES 4 SERVINGS.

PER SERVING *303 cal., 11 g fat (3 g sat. fat), 60 mg chol., 622 mg sodium, 27 g carb., 2 g fiber, 22 g pro.*

TUSCAN LAMB CHOP SKILLET

START TO FINISH **20 minutes**

8 lamb rib chops, cut 1 inch thick (1½ lb. total)

2 tsp. olive oil

3 cloves garlic, minced

1 15- to 19-oz. can cannellini beans (white kidney beans), rinsed and drained

1 8-oz. can Italian-style stewed tomatoes, undrained

1 Tbsp. balsamic vinegar

2 tsp. snipped fresh rosemary

    Fresh rosemary (optional)

EITHER LAMB RIB OR LOIN CHOPS WILL BE DELICIOUS IN THIS RECIPE. RIB CHOPS CONTAIN MORE FAT, WHICH CARRIES THE DISTINCTIVE FLAVOR LAMB ENTHUSIASTS LOVE. BOTH TYPES ARE EXCEPTIONALLY TENDER. LOOK FOR CHOPS WITH A LIGHT TO DARK PINK COLOR WITH WHITE FAT THAT HAS NO GRAY TONES.

1. Trim fat from lamb chops. In a large skillet heat oil over medium heat. Add chops; cook 8 minutes for medium (160°F), turning once. Remove chops from skillet; cover to keep warm.

2. Stir garlic into drippings in skillet. Cook and stir 1 minute. Stir in beans, tomatoes, vinegar, and the snipped rosemary. Bring to boiling; reduce heat. Simmer, uncovered, 3 minutes. Return lamb chops to skillet. If desired, sprinkle with additional fresh rosemary. **MAKES 4 SERVINGS.**

PER SERVING *272 cal., 9 g fat (3 g sat. fat), 67 mg chol., 466 mg sodium, 24 g carb., 6 g fiber, 30 g pro.*

HOT GINGERED BEEF AND BROCCOLI SALAD

START TO FINISH **20 minutes**

- 12 oz. boneless beef sirloin steak
- ⅔ cup bottled light ginger vinaigrette salad dressing
- 3 cups broccoli florets
- 8 cups mixed spring salad greens or baby salad greens
- 1 medium red sweet pepper, cut into bite-size strips

MAKE THIS QUICK HEALTHY DINNER EVEN SPEEDIER BY PURCHASING PRESLICED BEEF FOR STIR-FRYING.

1. Trim fat from meat. Thinly slice meat across the grain into bite-size strips.

2. In a large skillet or wok heat 2 Tbsp. of the salad dressing over medium-high heat. Add broccoli; cook and stir 3 minutes. Add meat; cook and stir 2 to 3 minutes more or until meat is slightly pink in center.

3. Transfer meat mixture to a large bowl; add salad greens and sweet pepper. Drizzle with the remaining salad dressing; toss gently to coat.

MAKES 4 SERVINGS.

PER SERVING *240 cal., 10 g fat (2 g sat. fat), 59 mg chol., 504 mg sodium, 13 g carb., 1 g fiber, 23 g pro.*

SWEET AND SPICY EDAMAME-BEEF STIR-FRY

START TO FINISH **30 minutes**

8 oz. boneless beef sirloin steak

4 tsp. vegetable oil

2 tsp. finely chopped fresh ginger

2 cups broccoli florets

1 cup red and/or yellow sweet pepper strips

1 cup frozen edamame

3 Tbsp. hoisin sauce

2 Tbsp. rice vinegar

1 tsp. red chili paste

2 cups hot cooked brown or white rice

THINLY SLICED LEAN SIRLOIN, QUICK-COOKING VEGGIES, AND FLAVORFUL AND CONVENIENT ASIAN CONDIMENTS TAKE THIS MEAL TO THE TABLE IN JUST 30 MINUTES.

1. Trim fat from meat. Thinly slice meat across the grain into bite-size strips.

2. In a nonstick wok or large skillet heat 2 tsp. of the oil over medium-high heat. Add ginger; cook and stir 15 seconds. Add broccoli and sweet pepper; cook and stir 4 minutes or until crisp-tender. Remove vegetables from wok.

3. Add remaining 2 tsp. oil to wok. Add beef and edamame; cook and stir over medium-high heat 2 minutes or until beef is desired doneness. Return vegetables to wok.

4. In a bowl stir together hoisin sauce, vinegar, and chili paste. Add to stir-fry, tossing to coat; heat through. Serve over rice. **MAKES 4 SERVINGS.**

PER SERVING *340 cal., 11 g fat (2 g sat. fat), 24 mg chol., 262 mg sodium, 38 g carb., 6 g fiber, 22 g pro.*

SOY-GLAZED FLANK STEAK STIR-FRY WITH BLISTERED GREEN BEANS

START TO FINISH **35 minutes**

1 lb. fresh green beans

1 lb. beef flank steak

6 cloves garlic, minced

1 Tbsp. minced fresh ginger

2 to 3 Tbsp. peanut oil

4 green onions (white parts only), sliced diagonally

2 Tbsp. sweet rice wine (mirin)

2 Tbsp. soy sauce

1 tsp. packed brown sugar

1 tsp. Asian chili paste (sambal oelek)

Sesame seeds, toasted (tip, page 15) (optional)

Snipped fresh herbs or chopped green onion tops (optional)

Hot cooked jasmine rice (optional)

WHEN SLICING FLANK STEAK, BE SURE TO CUT IT PERPENDICULARLY TO THE NATURAL GRAIN OF THE MEAT TO ENSURE EACH BITE WILL BE TENDER.

1. If desired, trim and cut green beans in half diagonally. Trim fat from meat. Thinly slice meat across the grain into bite-size strips. In a bowl combine garlic and ginger.

2. In an extra-large skillet or wok heat 2 Tbsp. of the oil over medium-high heat. Add green beans; cook and stir 7 to 8 minutes or until beans are blistered and brown in spots. Remove beans and drain on paper towels.

3. If necessary, add remaining 1 Tbsp. oil to hot skillet. Add garlic-ginger; cook and stir 30 seconds. Add half of the meat; cook and stir 3 minutes or until meat is slightly pink in center. Remove meat with a slotted spoon. Repeat with the remaining meat. Return all of the meat to skillet. Stir in sliced green onions, rice wine, soy sauce, brown sugar, and chili paste. Cook and stir 1 minute. Return green beans to skillet. Cook and stir 2 minutes more or until beans are heated through.

4. If desired, sprinkle stir-fry with sesame seeds and/or herbs and serve with hot cooked rice sprinkled with herbs. **MAKES 4 SERVINGS.**

PER SERVING *312 cal., 16 g fat (5 g sat. fat), 53 mg chol., 672 mg sodium, 15 g carb., 4 g fiber, 28 g pro.*

PORK STIR-FRY WITH CRISPY RICE NOODLES

START TO FINISH 30 minutes

½   cup reduced-sodium chicken broth

¼   cup sweet rice wine (mirin)

¼   cup reduced-sodium soy sauce

2   Tbsp. water

4   tsp. fish sauce

1   Tbsp. cornstarch

½ to 1 tsp. crushed red pepper

1   Tbsp. vegetable oil

1   tsp. grated fresh ginger

2   cloves garlic, minced

2   heads baby bok choy, halved or quartered (8 oz.)

1½ cups thinly sliced carrots

1½ cups fresh pea pods, tips and strings removed

1   large red sweet pepper, cut into bite-size strips

4   green onions, bias sliced

1   lb. boneless pork loin, trimmed of fat and cut into thin bite-size strips

Crispy rice noodles* or hot cooked rice

MIRIN IS A SWEET, LOW-ALCOHOL RICE WINE THAT ADDS A DISTINCT FLAVOR TO THE SAUCE FOR THIS STIR-FRY. IF IT'S NOT AVAILABLE, YOU CAN SUBSTITUTE SAKE WINE WITH AN ADDED PINCH OF SUGAR.

1. For sauce, in a bowl stir together the first seven ingredients (through crushed red pepper).
2. In an extra-large skillet or wok heat oil over medium-high heat. Add ginger and garlic; cook and stir 15 seconds. Add bok choy; cook 2 minutes. Add carrots; cook 2 minutes. Add pea pods, sweet pepper, and green onions; cook and stir 3 to 4 minutes or until vegetables are crisp-tender. Remove vegetables from the skillet.
3. Add half of the pork to hot skillet, adding more oil as necessary. Cook and stir 2 to 3 minutes or until pork is no longer pink. Remove from skillet. Repeat with remaining pork. Return all pork to skillet; push from center of skillet. Stir sauce; add to center of skillet. Cook and stir 1 to 2 minutes or until thickened and bubbly. Return vegetables to skillet; heat through. Serve with crispy rice noodles. **MAKES 4 SERVINGS.**

*Tip To make crispy rice noodles, use rice sticks (rice vermicelli). Separate the bundle of noodles into smaller portions. If desired, cut into 4- to 5-inch lengths. Add enough vegetable oil to a large skillet to fill to a depth of 1 inch. Heat oil (the oil is hot enough when a few noodles puff within seconds of being placed in the skillet.) Cook noodles in batches in the hot oil just until puffed. Remove noodles immediately and drain on paper towels.

PER SERVING *349 cal., 8 g fat (2 g sat. fat), 78 mg chol., 1,561 mg sodium, 37 g carb., 4 g fiber, 31 g pro.*

PORK LO MEIN

START TO FINISH **35 minutes**

12 oz. boneless pork loin, trimmed of fat and cut into thin bite-size strips

1 Tbsp. sesame seeds

1 Tbsp. grated fresh ginger

4 cloves garlic, minced

⅓ cup reduced-sodium chicken broth

3 Tbsp. reduced-sodium soy sauce

1 Tbsp. rice vinegar

1½ tsp. cornstarch

1 tsp. sugar

½ tsp. sriracha sauce

4 oz. dried Chinese egg noodles (lo mein noodles)

Nonstick cooking spray

1 cup sliced celery

1 medium red sweet pepper, cut into thin bite-size strips

3 cups coarsely shredded bok choy or napa cabbage

1 8-oz. can sliced bamboo shoots, rinsed and drained

6 Tbsp. thinly sliced green onions

2 tsp. toasted sesame oil

IF THERE ARE NO DIRECTIONS ON THE PACKAGE FOR COOKING THE NOODLES—OR IF THEY'RE WRITTEN IN AN UNFAMILIAR LANGUAGE—COOK THEM ABOUT 4 MINUTES OR UNTIL TENDER BUT STILL SLIGHTLY FIRM.

1. In a bowl combine meat, sesame seeds, ginger, and garlic. For sauce, in another bowl combine the next six ingredients (through sriracha sauce).

2. Cook noodles in boiling, lightly salted water according to package directions; drain. Rinse with cold water; drain again.

3. Coat a large skillet or wok with cooking spray; heat over medium-high heat. Add celery and sweet pepper; cook and stir 4 minutes. Add bok choy, bamboo shoots, and green onions; cook and stir 2 minutes. Remove vegetables from skillet.

4. Add sesame oil to skillet; add meat mixture. Cook and stir 2 to 3 minutes or until meat is no longer pink. Push from center of skillet. Stir sauce; add to center of skillet. Cook and stir 1 to 2 minutes or until thickened and bubbly. Stir in cooked noodles and vegetables. Cook and stir 2 minutes or until heated through. **MAKES 4 SERVINGS.**

PER SERVING *291 cal., 8 g fat (2 g sat. fat), 41 mg chol., 820 mg sodium, 31 g carb., 3 g fiber, 25 g pro.*

QUICK MU SHU PORK

12 oz. boneless pork top loin chops

1 Tbsp. vegetable oil

3 cups sliced fresh button mushrooms (8 oz.)

½ cup bias-sliced green onions

4 cups shredded cabbage with carrot (coleslaw mix)

2 Tbsp. soy sauce

1 tsp. toasted sesame oil

⅛ tsp. crushed red pepper

8 7- to 8-inch flour tortillas, warmed

¼ cup hoisin sauce or plum sauce

USE YOUR FAVORITE FLOUR TORTILLAS FOR THESE ASIAN-STYLE WRAPS. WHEAT, SPINACH, AND MULTIGRAIN TORTILLAS ARE DELICIOUS ALTERNATIVES TO REGULAR FLOUR TORTILLAS.

1. Trim fat from meat. Cut meat into thin strips. In a large skillet or wok heat vegetable oil over medium-high heat. Add meat; cook and stir 2 to 3 minutes or until slightly pink in center. Remove from skillet.

2. Add mushrooms and green onions to hot skillet. Cook 3 minutes or until mushrooms are tender, stirring occasionally. Add cabbage with carrot; cook and stir 1 minute or just until cabbage is wilted.

3. Return meat to skillet. Stir in soy sauce, sesame oil, and crushed red pepper; heat through. Serve with tortillas and hoisin sauce.

MAKES 4 SERVINGS.

PER SERVING *400 cal., 13 g fat (3 g sat. fat), 57 mg chol., 1,066 mg sodium, 43 g carb., 4 g fiber, 27 g pro.*

POTATO-CHORIZO SKILLET

START TO FINISH **45 minutes**

- 1 lb. tiny new potatoes
- 2 Tbsp. water
- 8 oz. uncooked Mexican chorizo, casings removed if present
- ⅓ cup chopped onion
- ½ cup chopped red and/or yellow sweet pepper
- ½ tsp. ground cumin

  Black pepper (optional)

MEXICAN CHORIZO IS UNCOOKED SAUSAGE MADE FROM GROUND FATTY PORK SEASONED WITH CHILE PEPPERS. LOOK FOR IT WITH OR WITHOUT CASINGS IN MEXICAN GROCERY STORES OR WITH THE OTHER SAUSAGE IN LARGER SUPERMARKETS.

1. Cut potatoes into uniform bite-size pieces. Place potatoes in a single layer in a baking dish; add the water. Microwave, loosely covered, 8 minutes or until potatoes are tender, stirring once. (Or in a large covered saucepan cook potatoes in enough boiling salted water to cover 10 minutes or until tender.) Drain.

2. In a large skillet cook chorizo over medium-high heat until no longer pink. Remove chorizo and drain on paper towels, reserving 1 Tbsp. drippings in skillet. Pat chorizo with paper towels to remove additional fat.

3. Add onion to the reserved drippings; cook 1 minute. Add cooked potatoes, sweet pepper, and cumin. Cook 8 minutes or until potatoes are golden brown and vegetables are tender, stirring frequently. Stir in chorizo; heat through. If desired, sprinkle with black pepper.

MAKES 6 SERVINGS.

PER SERVING *235 cal., 15 g fat (5 g sat. fat), 33 mg chol., 473 mg sodium, 15 g carb., 2 g fiber, 11 g pro.*

MEXICAN RICE AND BEAN SKILLET WITH CHORIZO

START TO FINISH **25 minutes**

12 oz. uncooked Mexican chorizo or pork sausage, casings removed if present

2 cups frozen whole kernel corn

1 14.5-oz. can diced tomatoes, undrained

1 cup uncooked instant rice

½ cup water

2 tsp. chili powder

½ tsp. ground cumin

1 15-oz. can pinto beans, rinsed and drained

¾ cup shredded Mexican-style four cheese blend or Colby and Monterey Jack cheese (3 oz.)

Shredded lettuce (optional)

Chopped fresh tomato (optional)

IF YOU PREFER, YOU CAN SWAP OUT THE PINTO BEANS FOR ANOTHER KIND OF CANNED BEANS, SUCH AS BLACK BEANS, KIDNEY BEANS, OR NAVY BEANS.

1. In a large skillet cook chorizo over medium heat until no longer pink. Remove chorizo and drain on paper towels. Drain fat from skillet.

2. In the same skillet combine the next six ingredients (through cumin). Bring to boiling; reduce heat. Simmer, covered, 5 minutes or until liquid is absorbed and rice is tender. Stir in beans and chorizo; heat through. Remove from heat.

3. Sprinkle with cheese. Cover and let stand 2 to 3 minutes or until cheese is slightly melted. If desired, top with lettuce and/or fresh tomato.

MAKES 6 SERVINGS.

PER SERVING *230 cal., 27 g fat (11 g sat. fat), 13 mg chol., 585 mg sodium, 38 g carb., 5 g fiber, 23 g pro.*

CREAMY STOVE-TOP ALFREDO WITH BACON AND PEAS

START TO FINISH **35 minutes**

4   slices thick-sliced bacon, coarsely chopped

2   cloves garlic, minced

8   oz. dried rotini, penne, or rigatoni pasta

1   14.5-oz. can chicken broth

1   cup water

½   tsp. salt

¼   tsp. freshly ground black pepper

1   cup frozen peas

¼   to ⅓ cup heavy cream

¼   cup grated Parmesan cheese

    Crisp-cooked bacon, crumbled (optional)

IN A PINCH, YOU CAN USE WHOLE MILK INSTEAD OF THE HEAVY CREAM—BUT YOU'LL MISS OUT ON SOME OF THE CREAMY GOODNESS.

1. In a large deep skillet cook the chopped bacon over medium heat until crisp. Add garlic; cook and stir 30 seconds. Drain off fat. Stir in pasta, broth, the water, salt, and pepper.

2. Bring to boiling; reduce heat. Simmer, covered, 12 to 15 minutes or until pasta is tender but still firm, stirring once. Stir in peas, heavy cream, and cheese. Cook and stir 2 minutes or until heated through. If desired, sprinkle with crumbled bacon. **MAKES 4 SERVINGS.**

PER SERVING *378 cal., 13 g fat (6 g sat. fat), 37 mg chol., 1,043 mg sodium, 49 g carb., 3 g fiber, 16 g pro.*

QUICK CHILI-PASTA SKILLET

PREP **15 minutes**

COOK **20 minutes**

STAND **2 minutes**

1   lb. lean ground beef

¾   cup chopped onion

1   15-oz. can red kidney, black, or red beans, rinsed and drained

1   14.5-oz. can diced tomatoes, undrained

1   8-oz. can tomato sauce

½   cup dried elbow macaroni

1   4-oz. can diced green chile peppers, drained

2   to 3 tsp. chili powder

½   tsp. garlic salt

½   cup shredded Monterey Jack or cheddar cheese (2 oz.)

THIS KID-FRIENDLY DINNER IS PERFECT FOR A BUSY WEEKNIGHT. IF YOU DON'T HAVE ELBOW MACARONI IN YOUR CUPBOARD, ANOTHER SHAPE OF PASTA—SUCH AS SHELLS, BOW TIES, OR WAGON WHEELS—WILL WORK JUST AS WELL.

1. In a large skillet cook ground beef and onion over medium-high heat until meat is browned. Drain off fat.

2. Stir in the next seven ingredients (through garlic salt). Bring to boiling; reduce heat. Simmer, covered, 20 minutes or until macaroni is tender but still firm, stirring frequently. Remove from heat.

3. Sprinkle chili-pasta with cheese. Cover and let stand 2 minutes or until cheese is melted.

MAKES 6 SERVINGS.

PER SERVING *289 cal., 11 g fat (5 g sat. fat), 56 mg chol., 622 mg sodium, 27 g carb., 5 g fiber, 23 g pro.*

PIZZA-PASTA SKILLET CASSEROLE

PREP 35 minutes

BAKE 35 minutes at 350°F

2 cups dried cavatappi pasta

1 3½-oz. pkg. thinly sliced pepperoni

1 lb. lean ground beef

⅓ cup finely chopped onion

1 8-oz. pkg. mushrooms, sliced

1 15-oz. can pizza sauce

1 8-oz. can tomato sauce

1 6-oz. can tomato paste

½ tsp. sugar

⅛ tsp. black pepper

⅛ tsp. garlic salt

⅛ tsp. onion salt

2 cups shredded mozzarella cheese

1 Tbsp. grated Parmesan cheese

THIS RECIPE IS VERY FLEXIBLE. IF YOU LIKE, ADD OR SUBSTITUTE OTHER FAVORITE PIZZA TOPPINGS. TRY COOKING CHOPPED SWEET PEPPERS WITH THE BEEF AND ONION, OR STIR IN SLICED BLACK OLIVES WITH THE PEPPERONI. OR YOU CAN SUBSTITUTE SWEET OR HOT ITALIAN SAUSAGE FOR THE GROUND BEEF.

1. Preheat oven to 350°F. Cook pasta according to package directions, except omit salt; drain. Return pasta to pot. Meanwhile, cut three-fourths of the pepperoni slices in quarters.

2. In a large oven-going skillet cook ground beef, onion, and mushrooms until meat is browned and onion is tender; drain off fat. Stir in the reserved pepperoni slices and next seven ingredients (through onion salt). Add to pasta.

3. Return half of the pasta mixture to the skillet. Sprinkle with half the mozzarella cheese. Repeat layers. Top with the reserved whole pepperoni slices and sprinkle with Parmesan cheese.

4. Bake 35 minutes or until heated through and cheese and pepperoni are lightly browned.

MAKES 8 SERVINGS.

PER SERVING *387 cal., 19 g fat (8 g sat. fat), 67 mg chol., 916 mg sodium, 29 g carb., 3 g fiber, 28 g pro.*

SKILLET CALZONE

PREP **30 minutes**
BAKE **25 minutes at 400°F**
STAND **5 minutes**

1 lb. ground beef or ground turkey

¼ cup chopped onion

1 lb. fresh or frozen pizza dough, thawed

½ cup marinara sauce

2 cups shredded mozzarella cheese or Italian blend cheeses (8 oz.)

1 cup sliced fresh mushrooms

1 cup chopped red, yellow, and/or green sweet peppers

½ tsp. dried oregano, crushed

¼ to ½ tsp. crushed red pepper

Grated Parmesan cheese (optional)

Snipped fresh Italian parsley (optional)

Marinara sauce, warmed

YOU CAN SUB IN OTHER FUN PIZZA TOPPINGS—SUCH AS OLIVES, ARTICHOKE HEARTS, CHOPPED PINEAPPLE, OR BANANA PEPPERS—FOR THE MUSHROOMS AND SWEET PEPPERS.

1. Preheat oven to 400°F. In a large heavy oven-going skillet cook ground beef and onion over medium-high heat until meat is browned and onion is tender. Transfer meat mixture to a paper towel to drain. Wipe out skillet with a paper towel; cool slightly.

2. On a lightly floured surface, divide pizza dough in half. Roll one dough portion into a 12-inch circle. Press onto the bottom and up the sides of the skillet. Spread the ½ cup marinara sauce over dough. Top with meat, mozzarella cheese, mushrooms, sweet peppers, oregano, and crushed red pepper. Roll the remaining dough portion into an 11-inch circle; place on top of filling. Pinch edges of bottom and top crusts together to seal. Using a sharp knife, cut slits in top crust.

3. Bake 25 minutes or until crust is golden brown and filling is bubbly. Let stand 5 minutes before serving. If desired, sprinkle with Parmesan cheese and/or parsley. Cut into wedges and serve with additional warmed marinara sauce. **MAKES 6 SERVINGS.**

PER SERVING *498 cal., 22 g fat (9 g sat. fat), 73 mg chol., 782 mg sodium, 42 g carb., 3 g fiber, 32 g pro.*

POULTRY

LEMON-BUTTER CHICKEN BREASTS

START TO FINISH 30 minutes

6   skinless, boneless chicken breast halves (1½ to 2 lb. total)

½   cup all-purpose flour

½   tsp. salt

2   tsp. lemon-pepper seasoning

⅓   cup butter

2   lemons, sliced

2   Tbsp. lemon juice

    Hot cooked rice (optional)

BY ADDING THE ENTIRE SLICED LEMON TO THE SKILLET, THE CHICKEN BREASTS TAKE ON THE FLAVORS OF BOTH THE TANGY JUICE AND FRAGRANT ZEST.

1. Place each chicken breast half between two pieces of plastic wrap. Using the flat side of a meat mallet, pound chicken lightly until ¼ inch thick. Discard plastic wrap. In a shallow dish stir together flour and salt. Dip chicken into flour mixture, turning to coat. Sprinkle chicken with lemon-pepper seasoning.

2. In an extra-large skillet cook chicken, half at a time, in hot butter over medium-high heat 6 minutes or until chicken is no longer pink, turning once. Remove chicken from skillet. Add lemon slices to skillet; cook 2 to 3 minutes or until lightly browned, turning once.

3. Return chicken to skillet, overlapping pieces slightly and arranging lemon slices around chicken. Drizzle with lemon juice. Cook 2 to 3 minutes or until pan juices are reduced slightly. Transfer chicken and lemon slices to a serving platter. Pour pan juices over chicken. If desired, serve with hot cooked rice. **MAKES 6 SERVINGS.**

PER SERVING *258 cal., 12 g fat (7 g sat. fat), 95 mg chol., 725 mg sodium, 8 g carb., 0 g fiber, 27 g pro.*

CHICKEN WITH PAN SAUCE 4 WAYS

START TO FINISH **35 minutes**

- 4 skinless, boneless chicken breast halves (about 4 oz. each)
- ¼ tsp. salt
- ¼ tsp. freshly ground black pepper
- 1 Tbsp. olive oil
- ½ cup dry white wine or chicken broth
- ½ cup chicken broth
- ¼ cup finely chopped shallot or onion

  Sauce Add-In
- 2 Tbsp. heavy cream
- ¼ cup cold butter

IF THE CHICKEN STICKS TO THE SKILLET A LITTLE WHILE COOKING, DON'T WORRY—THE BROWNED BITS LEFT IN THE SKILLET GIVE THE FINISHED SAUCE A DELICIOUS CARAMELIZED FLAVOR.

1. Place each chicken breast between two pieces of plastic wrap. Using the flat side of a meat mallet, pound chicken lightly until about ¼ inch thick. Discard plastic wrap. Sprinkle chicken with salt and pepper.

2. In an extra-large skillet heat oil over medium-high heat. Add chicken to skillet; cook 5 to 6 minutes or until no longer pink, turning once. Remove chicken from skillet; keep warm. Remove skillet from heat.

3. For sauce, add wine, broth, shallot, and desired Sauce Add-In (right) to the hot skillet. Return skillet to heat. Cook and stir to scrape up the browned bits from the bottom of the skillet. Bring to boiling. Boil gently, uncovered, 10 minutes or until liquid is reduced to ¼ cup. Reduce heat to medium-low.

4. Stir in cream. Add butter, 1 Tbsp. at a time, stirring until butter melts after each addition. Sauce should be slightly thickened. Season to taste with additional salt and pepper. Serve sauce over chicken. **MAKES 4 SERVINGS.**

CHICKEN WITH MUSHROOM PAN SAUCE
Prepare as directed, except add 1 cup assorted sliced fresh mushrooms to skillet with shallot. Cook until tender and golden. Add wine and broth; continue as directed.

CHICKEN WITH TOMATO-PARMESAN PAN SAUCE Prepare as directed, except add ½ cup quartered grape tomatoes to skillet with shallot. Stir 2 Tbsp. grated Parmesan cheese into finished sauce.

CHICKEN WITH BALSAMIC-CAPER PAN SAUCE Prepare as directed, except stir 2 tsp. balsamic vinegar and 2 tsp. drained and rinsed capers into finished sauce.

CHICKEN WITH BACON-LEEK PAN SAUCE
Prepare as directed, except add ½ cup sliced leek to skillet with shallot. Stir 3 slices crumbled crisp-cooked bacon into finished sauce.

PER SERVING *287 cal., 20 g fat (10 g sat. fat), 96 mg chol., 458 mg sodium, 3 g carb., 0 g fiber, 19 g pro.*

CHICKEN, BACON, AND VEGGIE SKILLET

START TO FINISH 45 minutes

1 lb. asparagus spears trimmed and cut in half, or green beans

4 slices bacon, coarsely chopped

4 skinless, boneless chicken breast halves (about 1½ lb. total)

   Salt

   Black pepper

1 medium yellow summer squash, halved lengthwise and cut into ½-inch slices

1 14.5-oz. can chicken broth

2 Tbsp. all-purpose flour

½ tsp. lemon zest

   Lemon wedges

IF YOU LIKE, USE 1½ CUPS CHICKEN BROTH AND ¼ CUP DRY, CRISP WHITE WINE IN PLACE OF THE CAN OF CHICKEN BROTH. CHOOSE A PINOT GRIGIO, SAUVIGNON BLANC, OR UNOAKED CHARDONNAY.

1. In a large saucepan cook asparagus in a small amount of boiling water 3 minutes or until crisp-tender; drain. Immediately plunge into ice water to stop cooking.

2. In an extra-large skillet cook bacon over medium heat until crisp. Using a slotted spoon, remove bacon and drain on paper towels, reserving 1 tablespoon drippings in skillet.

3. Sprinkle chicken with salt and pepper. Cook chicken in reserved drippings over medium-high heat 12 minutes, turning once. Remove chicken from skillet; keep warm.

4. Add squash to skillet; cook 3 minutes, stirring occasionally. In a bowl whisk together broth, flour, and lemon zest; add to squash in skillet. Cook and stir until thickened and bubbly. Stir in asparagus and chicken. Cook 6 minutes more or until chicken is done (165°F). Sprinkle with reserved bacon. Serve with lemon wedges. **MAKES 4 SERVINGS.**

PER SERVING *272 cal., 11 g total fat (3 g sat. fat), 105 mg chol., 891 mg sodium, 8 g carb., 2 g fiber, 3 g sugar, 36 g pro.*

LEMON-THYME ROASTED CHICKEN WITH FINGERLINGS

START TO FINISH **30 minutes**

4 tsp. canola oil or olive oil

1 tsp. dried thyme, crushed

½ tsp. kosher salt or ¼ tsp. regular salt

¼ tsp. freshly ground black pepper

1 lb. fingerling potatoes, halved lengthwise or small new red or Yukon gold potatoes, halved

4 skinless, boneless chicken breast halves (1 to 1¼ lb. total)

2 cloves garlic, minced

1 lemon, thinly sliced

Snipped fresh thyme (optional)

FINGERLING POTATOES ARE SMALL, FINGER-SHAPE POTATOES THAT HAVE A RICH, BUTTERY TEXTURE. THEY ARE AVAILABLE IN A VARIETY OF COLORS—FROM GOLD TO DEEP PURPLE.

1. In an extra-large skillet heat 2 tsp. of the oil over medium heat. Stir in ½ tsp. of the dried thyme, the salt, and pepper. Add potatoes; toss gently to coat. Cook, covered, 12 minutes, stirring twice.

2. Stir potatoes; push to one side of skillet. Add the remaining 2 tsp. oil to the other side of skillet. Arrange chicken in skillet alongside the potatoes. Cook, uncovered, 5 minutes.

3. Turn chicken. Sprinkle with garlic and the remaining ½ tsp. dried thyme; top with lemon slices. Cook, covered, 7 to 10 minutes more or until chicken is no longer pink (170°F) and potatoes are tender. If desired, sprinkle with fresh thyme. **MAKES 4 SERVINGS.**

PER SERVING *255 cal., 6 g fat (1 g sat. fat), 66 mg chol., 307 mg sodium, 21 g carb., 3 g fiber, 29 g pro.*

ALMOND-CRUSTED CHICKEN

START TO FINISH **35 minutes**

- 4 skinless, boneless chicken breast halves (1 to 1¼ lb. total)
- 1 egg, lightly beaten
- 2 Tbsp. buttermilk
- ½ cup finely chopped almonds
- ½ cup panko bread crumbs or fine dry bread crumbs
- 2 tsp. snipped fresh rosemary
- ½ tsp. salt
- 1 Tbsp. peanut oil or canola oil
- 2 Tbsp. sliced shallot
- 8 cups fresh spinach leaves
  Freshly ground black pepper
  Fresh mint leaves (optional)

BE SURE THE ALMONDS ARE CHOPPED FINELY AND EVENLY SO THEY CLING TO THE CHICKEN AND DON'T FALL OFF DURING COOKING. THE PIECES SHOULD BE NO BIGGER THAN ⅛ INCH.

1. Place each chicken breast half between two pieces of plastic wrap. Using the flat side of a meat mallet, pound chicken lightly until ¼ to ½ inch thick. Discard plastic wrap.

2. In a shallow dish combine egg and buttermilk. In another shallow dish stir together almonds, panko, rosemary, and ¼ tsp. of the salt. Dip chicken into egg mixture, then into almond mixture, turning to coat.

3. In an extra-large nonstick skillet cook chicken, half at a time if necessary, in hot oil over medium heat 4 to 6 minutes or until no longer pink, turning once. Remove chicken, reserving drippings in skillet. Keep chicken warm.

4. In the same skillet cook shallot in the reserved drippings 3 to 5 minutes or just until tender, stirring frequently. Add spinach and remaining ¼ tsp. salt; cook and toss about 1 minute or just until spinach is wilted. Season chicken and wilted spinach with pepper and, if desired, top with mint. **MAKES 4 SERVINGS.**

PER SERVING *276 cal., 11 g fat (1 g sat. fat), 66 mg chol., 456 mg sodium, 11 g carb., 3 g fiber, 33 g pro.*

CHICKEN IN SPICED ANCHO-PEANUT SAUCE

PREP 30 minutes

COOK 30 minutes

1 large dried ancho chile pepper, stemmed and seeded (tip, page 51)

6 bone-in chicken thighs, skinned if desired

Salt

Black pepper

¼ cup vegetable oil

½ cup chopped onion

3 cloves garlic, minced

1 14.5-oz. can fire-roasted diced tomatoes, drained

1 cup chicken broth

½ cup dry-roasted peanuts

1 tsp. ground cinnamon

¼ cup fresh cilantro sprigs

Hot cooked rice (optional)

THE POBLANO IS A MILD CHILE PEPPER. DRIED, IT'S CALLED ANCHO CHILE PEPPER AND ADDS A FRUITY, SLIGHTLY SMOKY FLAVOR.

1. In a bowl combine ancho chile pepper and enough hot water to cover. Let stand 15 minutes; drain and pat dry with paper towels. Cut into small pieces.

2. Meanwhile, lightly sprinkle chicken with salt and black pepper. In a large skillet cook chicken in hot oil over medium to medium-high heat 6 to 8 minutes or until golden brown, turning once. Remove chicken, reserving 2 Tbsp. oil in skillet.

3. Add onion, garlic, and ancho pepper pieces to skillet. Cook over medium heat 5 minutes or until onion is tender, stirring occasionally.

4. Transfer onion mixture to a food processor or blender. Cover and process or blend until a smooth paste forms. Add tomatoes, broth, peanuts, and cinnamon. Cover and process or blend until smooth. Return sauce to skillet; add chicken.

5. Bring to boiling; reduce heat. Simmer, uncovered, 30 minutes, turning chicken once. Top with cilantro and, if desired, additional peanuts. If desired, serve with hot cooked rice.

MAKES 6 SERVINGS.

PER SERVING *389 cal., 30 g fat (6 g sat. fat), 80 mg chol., 449 mg sodium, 11 g carb., 3 g fiber, 21 g pro.*

SEARED CHICKEN WITH CHERRY-TARRAGON SAUCE

START TO FINISH **30 minutes**

- ¼ cup all-purpose flour
- 2 tsp. smoked paprika
- 1 tsp. dry mustard
- ¼ tsp. salt
- ¼ tsp. black pepper
- 8 skinless, boneless chicken thighs
- 2 Tbsp. olive oil
- 2 cups frozen pitted dark sweet cherries, thawed
- 2 Tbsp. snipped fresh tarragon
- 3 cloves garlic, minced
- 1 cup dry red wine or cherry juice
- ½ cup chicken broth
- 2 Tbsp. butter

  Salt

  Black pepper
- 2 cups hot cooked couscous, rice, or pasta

SMOKED PAPRIKA GIVES THE CHICKEN A SUBTLE, SMOKY FLAVOR. IF YOU PREFER, YOU CAN SUBSTITUTE REGULAR SWEET PAPRIKA.

1. In a shallow dish combine the first five ingredients (through pepper). Dip chicken in flour mixture, turning to coat. In an extra-large skillet cook chicken in hot oil over medium to medium-high heat 8 to 10 minutes or until chicken is done (170°F), turning once. Remove from skillet; cover to keep warm.

2. Add cherries, tarragon, and garlic to the same skillet. Cook and stir over medium heat 1 minute. Stir in wine and broth. Simmer, uncovered, 3 to 5 minutes or until sauce is reduced to about 2 cups. Add butter, stirring until melted. Season to taste with additional salt and pepper.

3. Spoon sauce over chicken and serve with couscous. If desired, sprinkle with additional fresh tarragon. **MAKES 4 SERVINGS.**

PER SERVING *573 cal., 21 g fat (7 g sat. fat), 180 mg chol., 631 mg sodium, 40 g carb., 3 g fiber, 44 g pro.*

CHICKEN AND LENTILS IN APPLE-CURRY SAUCE

PREP 25 minutes

COOK 40 minutes

- 2 Tbsp. olive oil
- 6 skinless, boneless chicken thighs
- 1 large yellow onion, halved and thinly sliced
- 1 Tbsp. grated fresh ginger
- 4 cloves garlic, minced
- 2 Tbsp. tomato paste
- 1 Tbsp. mild curry powder
- 1 tsp. salt
- 1 tsp. garam masala
- 3 cups reduced-sodium chicken broth
- 1½ cups lentils, rinsed and drained
- 3 medium red and/or green cooking apples, cored and cut into 1-inch pieces
- 2 5-oz. pkg. fresh baby spinach

    Plain yogurt (optional)

    Sliced green onions (optional)

THIS SAVORY-SWEET DISH CALLS FOR TWO TYPES OF CURRY POWDER: MILD CURRY AND GARAM MASALA. EACH INCLUDES A COMBINATION OF SPICES. AS WITH ALL GROUND SPICES, CURRY POWDER LOSES ITS FLAVOR OVER TIME. STORE IT IN A COOL, DRY PLACE OUT OF DIRECT SUNLIGHT FOR NO MORE THAN 6 MONTHS.

1. In an extra-large skillet heat oil over medium-high heat. Add chicken; cook 4 to 6 minutes or until browned, turning once. Remove chicken from skillet.

2. Add onion to skillet; cook over medium heat 3 minutes, stirring occasionally. Add ginger and garlic; cook and stir 1 minute more. Stir in tomato paste, curry powder, salt, and garam masala. Add broth and lentils; return chicken to skillet. Bring to boiling; reduce heat. Simmer, covered, 30 minutes.

3. Add apples to skillet. Simmer, covered, 10 minutes more or until lentils are tender. Gradually stir in about 3 cups of the spinach.

4. Divide remaining spinach among shallow bowls. Add chicken and lentil mixture. If desired, top with yogurt and sprinkle with green onions. **MAKES 6 SERVINGS.**

PER SERVING *383 cal., 8 g fat (1 g sat. fat), 66 mg chol., 812 mg sodium, 49 g carb., 19 g fiber, 30 g pro.*

LEMON-GINGER CHICKEN THIGHS

START TO FINISH 30 minutes

1 lemon

1 Tbsp. grated fresh ginger

½ tsp. salt

2 Tbsp. honey

2 Tbsp. water

1 Tbsp. reduced-sodium soy sauce

8 bone-in chicken thighs

2 tsp. vegetable oil

Sliced green onions (optional)

Lemon wedges (optional)

MAKE EASY WORK OF GRATING THE FRESH GINGER BY FREEZING IT FIRST. THEN KEEP THE REMAINING ROOT ON HAND IN THE FREEZER FOR UP TO 3 MONTHS, USING IT JUST AS YOU NEED IT.

1. Remove 1 Tbsp. zest and 2 Tbsp. juice lemon. In a bowl combine lemon zest, ginger, and salt. In another bowl combine lemon juice, honey, the water, and soy sauce.

2. Rub lemon zest mixture under the skin of the chicken thighs. In an extra-large skillet heat oil over medium-high heat. Add chicken, skin sides down; cook 7 minutes or until browned. Turn chicken; add lemon juice mixture. Reduce heat. Cook, covered, 14 to 18 minutes or until done (170°F).

3. If desired, skim fat from pan juices and drizzle juices over chicken. If desired, sprinkle with green onions and serve with lemon wedges. **MAKES 4 SERVINGS.**

PER SERVING *459 cal., 31 g fat (8 g sat. fat), 158 mg chol., 567 mg sodium, 12 g carb., 1 g fiber, 33 g pro.*

CHICKEN CACCIATORE

PREP 30 minutes

COOK 20 minutes

8 small chicken thighs (about 2 lb. total), skin removed

Salt

Cracked black pepper

1 Tbsp. olive oil

3 cups sliced fresh cremini mushrooms

1 large yellow or green sweet pepper, cut into bite-size strips

⅓ cup finely chopped carrot

3 cloves garlic, minced

½ cup dry white wine or chicken broth

1 28-oz. can diced tomatoes, undrained

1½ cups frozen small whole onions

1 tsp. dried oregano, crushed

1 tsp. coarse ground black pepper

2 Tbsp. balsamic vinegar

10 pitted Kalamata olives, chopped, if desired (optional)

⅓ cup snipped fresh Italian parsley (optional)

THE WORD CACCIATORE MEANS HUNTER IN ITALIAN, NAMED IN HONOR OF THE HUNTER'S WIFE WHO MIGHT COOK THE DISH ON THE EVE OF THE HUNT AS FUEL FOR THE CHASE. THIS SKILLET-COOKED VERSION INCLUDES THE TRADITIONAL COMBINATION OF SWEET PEPPERS, MUSHROOMS, AND OLIVES.

1. Sprinkle chicken lightly with salt and cracked black pepper. In a large skillet heat oil over medium heat. Add chicken; cook just until browned on both sides. Remove chicken from skillet.

2. Add mushrooms, sweet pepper, carrot, and garlic to skillet; cook and stir 4 minutes. Carefully add wine. Simmer, uncovered, until liquid is nearly evaporated. Stir in tomatoes, onions, oregano, and black pepper. Return chicken to skillet.

3. Bring to boiling; reduce heat. Simmer, covered, 15 minutes or until chicken is no longer pink (175°F). Stir in balsamic vinegar. Season to taste with additional salt. If desired, sprinkle with olives and parsley before serving.

MAKES 4 SERVINGS.

PER SERVING *317 cal., 9 g fat (2 g sat. fat), 129 mg chol., 609 mg sodium, 23 g carb., 4 g fiber, 31 g pro.*

GREEN CHILE FRIED CHICKEN

PREP 25 minutes

MARINATE 8 hours

COOK 35 minutes

A CAST-IRON SKILLET IS THE PERFECT TOOL FOR FRYING CHICKEN. ITS HEAVY WEIGHT ENABLES IT TO MAINTAIN AN EVEN TEMPERATURE DURING COOKING, RESULTING IN A CRISPY, GOLDEN BROWN CRUST.

1   2½- to 3-lb. cut-up broiler-fryer chicken, skinned if desired

1   8-oz. carton sour cream

1   4-oz. can diced green chile peppers, undrained

¼   cup milk

2   Tbsp. snipped fresh cilantro

2   Tbsp. lime juice

¾   tsp. ground cumin

1   clove garlic, minced

½   tsp. salt

¼   tsp. black pepper

¾   cup all-purpose flour

    Vegetable oil

    Lime wedges (optional)

    Sliced pickled jalapeño peppers (optional)

    Hot pepper sauce (optional)

1. Place chicken in a resealable plastic bag set in a shallow dish. For marinade, in a bowl combine the next nine ingredients (through black pepper). Pour marinade over chicken. Seal bag; turn to coat chicken. Marinate in the refrigerator 8 to 24 hours, turning bag occasionally. Drain chicken; discard marinade. **2.** Place flour in a shallow dish. Dip chicken into flour, turning to coat.

3. Meanwhile, in an extra-large heavy skillet heat ¼ to ½ inch oil to 350°F over medium-high heat. Reduce heat to medium. Carefully add chicken to skillet. Cook 35 minutes or until chicken is no longer pink (165°F for breasts; 170°F for thighs and drumsticks), turning occasionally. Remove chicken; drain on paper towels.

4. If desired, serve chicken with lime wedges, pickled jalapeño peppers, and/or hot pepper sauce. **MAKES 4 SERVINGS.**

PER SERVING *608 cal., 42 g fat (14 g sat. fat), 125 mg chol., 501 mg sodium, 22 g carb., 1 g fiber, 36 g pro.*

CHICKEN TACOS

START TO FINISH 30 minutes

Nonstick cooking spray

½ cup chopped onion

1 clove garlic, minced

2 cups shredded cooked chicken

1 8-oz. can tomato sauce

1 4-oz. can diced green chile peppers, drained

12 6-inch flour tortillas or taco shells

2 cups shredded lettuce

½ cup seeded and chopped tomato

½ cup finely shredded reduced-fat cheddar and/or Monterey Jack cheese (2 oz.)

Lime wedges

IF YOU DON'T HAVE LEFTOVER CHICKEN ON HAND, PICK UP A ROTISSERIE CHICKEN FROM YOUR SUPERMARKET TO USE IN THESE QUICK WEEKNIGHT TACOS.

1. Lightly coat a large nonstick skillet with cooking spray; heat skillet over medium heat. Add onion and garlic; cook until onion is tender, stirring occasionally. Stir in chicken, tomato sauce, and green chile peppers; heat through.

2. Divide chicken filling among tortillas. Top with lettuce, tomato, and cheese; fold sides over filling. Serve with lime wedges. **MAKES 12 TACOS.**

PER 2 TACOS *282 cal., 9 g fat (3 g sat. fat), 48 mg chol., 714 mg sodium, 31 g carb., 2 g fiber, 20 g pro.*

EASY CHICKEN JAMBALAYA

START TO FINISH 25 minutes

8 oz. skinless, boneless chicken breast halves, cut into 1-inch pieces

2 tsp. Cajun seasoning

8 oz. cooked spicy or mild sausage, sliced

2 medium yellow, green, and/or orange sweet peppers, cut into bite-size strips

1 small red onion, cut into thin wedges

2 14.5-oz. cans no-salt-added stewed tomatoes, undrained

Coarsely snipped fresh Italian parsley (optional)

CUT YOUR PREP TIME IN HALF BY BUYING CLEANED, PRECUT PEPPERS AND ONIONS IN YOUR SUPERMARKET'S PRODUCE SECTION AND CUT-UP, READY-TO-USE CHICKEN BREAST IN THE MEAT SECTION.

1. In a bowl combine chicken and Cajun seasoning; toss gently to coat.

2. Heat an extra-large skillet over medium-high heat. Add chicken and sausage; cook 3 to 4 minutes or until chicken begins to brown, stirring frequently. Add sweet peppers and onion; cook 2 minutes more.

3. Add stewed tomatoes, breaking up large pieces of tomato with a spoon. Cook, covered, 5 to 7 minutes or until chicken is no longer pink. If desired, sprinkle with parsley. **MAKES 4 SERVINGS.**

PER SERVING *355 cal., 18 g fat (5 g sat. fat), 81 mg chol., 637 mg sodium, 23 g carb., 3 g fiber, 29 g pro.*

HERBED CHICKEN, ORZO, AND ZUCCHINI

START TO FINISH **20 minutes**

1 cup dried orzo pasta (rosamarina)

4 skinless, boneless chicken breast halves (1 to 1¼ lb. total)

1 tsp. dried basil, crushed

3 Tbsp. olive oil

2 medium zucchini and/or yellow summer squash, halved lengthwise and sliced

2 Tbsp. red wine vinegar

1 Tbsp. snipped fresh dill weed

¼ tsp. salt

¼ tsp. black pepper

IF YOU PREFER TO USE A FRESH HERB OTHER THAN DILL, FRESH BASIL, PARSLEY, MINT, OR THYME MAKE FINE SUBSTITUTES.

1. Cook orzo according to package directions; drain. Return orzo to pan; cover and keep warm.
2. Meanwhile, sprinkle chicken with basil. In a large skillet heat 1 Tbsp. of the oil over medium-high heat. Add chicken; cook 10 minutes or until no longer pink (165°F), turning once. Remove chicken from skillet.

3. Add zucchini and/or yellow squash to skillet; cook and stir 3 minutes or until crisp-tender. Stir in cooked orzo, the remaining 2 Tbsp. oil, and the remaining ingredients.
4. Serve chicken with orzo mixture. If desired, sprinkle with additional fresh dill. **MAKES 4 SERVINGS.**

PER SERVING *390 cal., 12 g fat (2 g sat. fat), 66 mg chol., 366 mg sodium, 35 g carb., 3 g fiber, 33 g pro.*

STOVE-TOP CHICKEN, MACARONI, AND CHEESE

START TO FINISH 35 minutes

6 oz. dried multigrain or regular elbow macaroni

Nonstick cooking spray

12 oz. skinless, boneless chicken breast halves, cut into 1-inch pieces

¼ cup finely chopped onion

1 6.5-oz. pkg. light semisoft cheese with garlic and fines herbes

1⅔ cups fat-free milk

1 Tbsp. all-purpose flour

¾ cup shredded reduced-fat cheddar cheese (3 oz.)

2 cups fresh baby spinach

1 cup cherry tomatoes, quartered

SEMISOFT CHEESE SEASONED WITH HERBS AND GARLIC GIVES THIS DRESSED-UP MACARONI AND CHEESE A CREAMY TEXTURE AND PLENTY OF FLAVOR WITHOUT ADDING A LOT OF FAT.

1. Cook macaroni according to package directions, except do not add salt to the water; drain.

2. Meanwhile, coat a large nonstick skillet with cooking spray; heat skillet over medium-high heat. Add chicken and onion; cook 4 to 6 minutes or until chicken is no longer pink and onion is tender, stirring frequently. Remove from heat. Stir in semisoft cheese until melted.

3. In a bowl whisk together milk and flour until smooth. Gradually stir milk mixture into chicken mixture. Cook and stir over medium heat until thickened and bubbly. Reduce heat to low. Gradually add cheddar cheese, stirring until melted. Add cooked macaroni; cook and stir 1 to 2 minutes or until heated through. Stir in spinach. Top with cherry tomatoes. **MAKES 5 SERVINGS.**

PER SERVING *369 cal., 12 g fat (7 g sat. fat), 85 mg chol., 393 mg sodium, 33 g carb., 4 g fiber, 33 g pro.*

CHICKEN SPANAKOPITA SKILLET

PREP 30 minutes

BAKE 15 minutes at 375°F

- 4 tsp. olive oil
- ½ cup chopped onion
- 2 cloves garlic, minced
- ⅛ tsp. crushed red pepper
- ¼ cup heavy cream
- 2 5-oz. pkg. fresh baby spinach
- 1½ cups chopped rotisserie chicken
- ½ cup crumbled feta cheese (2 oz.)
- 2 Tbsp. snipped fresh Italian parsley
- 1 Tbsp. snipped fresh dill weed
- 5 sheets frozen phyllo dough (14×9-inch rectangles), thawed
- 2 Tbsp. butter, melted

SPANAKOPITA IS A SAVORY GREEK PIE MADE WITH PHYLLO DOUGH AND FILLED WITH SPINACH, FETA CHEESE, AND EGGS. THIS SKILLET VERSION FEATURES THE SAME MOUTHWATERING FLAVORS—PLUS CHICKEN—BUT IT'S MUCH EASIER AND FASTER TO PREPARE.

1. Preheat oven to 375°F. In a medium oven-going skillet heat 2 tsp. of the oil over medium-high heat. Add onion, garlic, and crushed red pepper; cook 3 to 4 minutes or until onion is tender, stirring occasionally. Stir in heavy cream; bring to boiling. Remove from heat.

2. In a 4- to 5-quart Dutch oven heat remaining 2 tsp. oil over medium-high heat. Add spinach; cook and stir 3 minutes or just until wilted. Drain spinach in a colander, pressing gently to remove excess liquid. Return spinach to Dutch oven. Stir in chicken, cheese, parsley, and dill. Stir spinach mixture into onion mixture.

3. Unfold phyllo dough; remove one sheet. (As you work, keep the remaining phyllo covered with plastic wrap to prevent it from drying out.) Brush phyllo sheet with some of the melted butter. Fold in half to make a 9×7-inch rectangle. Place on top of spinach mixture. Repeat with the remaining phyllo, brushing each sheet with butter and rotating slightly to stagger corners. (Phyllo sheets may tear a little.) Brush with any remaining butter. Cut a few slits in phyllo.

4. Bake 15 minutes or until top is golden. If desired, top with additional dill. **MAKES 6 SERVINGS.**

PER SERVING *282 cal., 17 g fat (8 g sat. fat), 96 mg chol., 491 mg sodium, 12 g carb., 2 g fiber, 20 g pro.*

SKILLET CHICKEN POT PIE

PREP **50 minutes**

BAKE **25 minutes at 400°F**

STAND **20 minutes**

1 recipe Pastry or ½ of a 14.1-oz. pkg. rolled refrigerated unbaked piecrust (1 crust)

2 Tbsp. butter

1 cup chopped onion

¾ cup sliced celery

½ cup chopped red sweet pepper

⅓ cup all-purpose flour

½ tsp. dried thyme, crushed

¼ tsp. salt

¼ tsp. black pepper

1½ cups chicken broth

1 cup half-and-half or milk

2½ cups chopped cooked chicken

1 cup frozen peas or frozen peas and carrots, thawed

1 egg

1 Tbsp. water

IF YOU'RE SHORT ON TIME, SKIP MAKING THE HOMEMADE PASTRY AND USE REFRIGERATED PIECRUST. PURCHASED PIE PASTRY HAS A TENDENCY TO TEAR WHEN DRAPED OVER THE SIDES, SO IF YOU OPT FOR THIS SHORTCUT, BE SURE TO TUCK THE EDGES OF THE PASTRY DOUGH INSIDE THE SKILLET BEFORE BAKING.

1. Prepare Pastry or allow refrigerated piecrust to stand according to package directions. Preheat oven to 400°F.

2. In a medium heavy oven-going skillet melt butter over medium heat. Add onion, celery, and sweet pepper; cook 4 to 5 minutes or until vegetables are tender, stirring occasionally. Stir in flour, thyme, salt, and black pepper. Gradually stir in broth and half-and-half. Cook and stir until thickened and bubbly. Stir in chicken and peas. Remove from heat.

3. On a lightly floured surface, roll pastry or refrigerated piecrust into a 13-inch circle. Using a sharp knife, cut slits in pastry or use a small cookie cutter to cut shapes from pastry.

4. Carefully place pastry circle over mixture in skillet, letting edges of pastry drape over the sides. Flute the edges of the pastry to the inside of the skillet. In a bowl beat together egg and the water. Brush pastry with some of the egg mixture. If using, place pastry cutouts on top of pastry and brush with beaten egg.

5. Place skillet in oven. Bake 25 to 30 minutes or until pastry is golden brown. Let stand 20 minutes before serving. **MAKES 6 SERVINGS.**

PASTRY In a bowl stir together 1½ cups all-purpose flour and ½ tsp. salt. Using a pastry blender, cut in ½ cup shortening until pieces are pea size. Sprinkle cold water, 1 Tbsp. at a time (¼ to ⅓ cup total), over part of the flour mixture; gently toss with a fork and push to side of bowl until moistened. Gather pastry into a ball, kneading gently until it holds together. Cover and chill until ready to use.

PER SERVING *537 cal., 31 g fat (11 g sat. fat), 109 mg chol., 657 mg sodium, 38 g carb., 3 g fiber, 25 g pro.*

CHICKEN MEATBALL NOODLE BOWL

START TO FINISH **25 minutes**

4 oz. dried thin rice noodles

12 oz. ground chicken

2 Tbsp. snipped fresh cilantro

1 Tbsp. grated fresh ginger

½ tsp. salt

3 Tbsp. olive oil or vegetable oil

1 fresh red Fresno chile pepper, seeded and finely chopped (tip, page 51)

⅓ cup rice vinegar

2 Tbsp. honey

1 Tbsp. lime juice

3 cups shredded leaf lettuce

½ cup finely shredded carrot

Fresh cilantro, sliced red Fresno chile peppers, sliced green onions, and/or lime wedges (optional)

THIS QUICK AND EASY NOODLE BOWL INCLUDES HOMEMADE CHICKEN MEATBALLS SEASONED SIMPLY WITH FRESH CILANTRO AND GINGER. IF GROUND CHICKEN ISN'T AVAILABLE YOU CAN USE GROUND TURKEY.

1. Prepare noodles according to package directions; drain.

2. Meanwhile, in a bowl combine the next four ingredients (through salt). Shape mixture into 16 meatballs.

3. In a large skillet heat 1 Tbsp. of the oil over medium heat. Add meatballs. Cook 10 minutes or until no longer pink (165°F), turning occasionally. Remove from heat. Remove meatballs from skillet.

4. For sauce, add the remaining 2 Tbsp. oil and the chopped chile pepper to skillet. Stir in vinegar, honey, and lime juice.

5. Divide lettuce among bowls. Top with noodles, carrot, and meatballs; drizzle with sauce. If desired, top with additional cilantro, sliced chile peppers, green onions, and/or lime wedges. **MAKES 4 SERVINGS.**

PER SERVING *369 cal., 17 g fat (3 g sat. fat), 73 mg chol., 414 mg sodium, 36 g carb., 1 g fiber, 16 g pro.*

CHICKEN CURRY SKILLET WITH RICE NOODLES

START TO FINISH **30 minutes**

- 8 oz. dried wide rice noodles, broken
- 2 Tbsp. vegetable oil
- 1½ lb. skinless, boneless chicken breast halves, cut into 1-inch pieces
- 1 16-oz. pkg. frozen desired stir-fry vegetables, thawed
- 1 14-oz. can unsweetened light coconut milk
- ½ cup water
- 1 Tbsp. sugar
- 1 Tbsp. fish sauce
- ½ to 1 tsp. red curry paste
- ¼ tsp. salt
- ¼ tsp. black pepper
- ¼ cup snipped fresh basil

LOOK FOR RICE NOODLES FOR THIS QUICK SKILLET IN THE ASIAN OR GLUTEN-FREE SECTIONS OF YOUR SUPERMARKET OR AT ASIAN GROCERY STORES.

1. Soak rice noodles according to package directions; drain.

2. In an extra-large skillet heat oil over medium-high heat. Add chicken; cook and stir 8 to 10 minutes or until chicken is no longer pink, adding stir-fry vegetables the last 4 minutes. Remove chicken mixture from skillet.

3. In the same skillet combine the next seven ingredients (through pepper). Bring to boiling. Stir in rice noodles and chicken mixture. Return to boiling; reduce heat. Simmer, uncovered, 2 minutes or until noodles are tender but still firm and sauce is thickened. Sprinkle with basil. **MAKES 6 SERVINGS.**

PER SERVING *386 cal., 10 g fat (3 g sat. fat), 66 mg chol., 529 mg sodium, 42 g carb., 2 g fiber, 28 g pro.*

THAI GREEN CHICKEN CURRY

START TO FINISH **35 minutes**

- 1 Tbsp. canola oil
- 3 cloves garlic, minced
- 1 cup unsweetened coconut milk
- ⅓ cup reduced-sodium chicken broth
- 1 Tbsp. fish sauce
- 2 tsp. packed brown sugar
- 2 Tbsp. green or yellow curry paste or 3 Tbsp. red curry paste
- 12 oz. skinless, boneless chicken thighs, trimmed of fat and cut into 1-inch strips
- 1 medium red or yellow sweet pepper, cut into thin bite-size strips
- ½ of a small eggplant, peeled, if desired, and cut into bite-size pieces (2 cups)
- ¼ cup thinly sliced fresh basil leaves
- 1 tsp. finely shredded lime peel
- 2 cups hot cooked jasmine rice*
  Fresh basil leaves
  Lime wedges

LOOK FOR FISH SAUCE, COCONUT MILK, JASMINE RICE, AND CURRY PASTE IN THE ASIAN SECTION OF LARGE SUPERMARKETS OR AT ASIAN FOOD STORES. BE SURE TO STIR THE COCONUT MILK IN THE CAN BEFORE MEASURING, AS THE SOLID AND LIQUID SEPARATE.

1. In a large nonstick skillet or wok heat oil over medium-high heat. Add garlic; cook 30 seconds. **2.** Stir in coconut milk, broth, fish sauce, and brown sugar. Whisk in curry paste. Bring to boiling; add chicken strips. Return to boiling; reduce heat. Boil gently, uncovered, 5 minutes, stirring occasionally. Stir in sweet pepper and eggplant. Continue to boil gently 5 minutes more or until chicken is no longer pink, vegetables are just tender, and sauce has thickened slightly, stirring occasionally. **3.** Remove from heat. Stir the ¼ cup thinly sliced basil leaves and the lime peel into chicken mixture. Serve over hot cooked rice. Top with fresh basil leaves and serve with lime wedges.
MAKES 4 SERVINGS.
*Tip For 2 cups cooked rice, in a medium saucepan combine 2 cups water, 1 cup uncooked jasmine rice, and, if desired, ½ tsp. salt. Bring to boiling; reduce heat. Simmer, covered, 20 minutes or until the liquid is absorbed and rice is tender.
PER SERVING *611 cal., 19 g fat (12 g sat. fat), 81 mg chol., 861 mg sodium, 84 g carb., 4 g fiber, 25 g pro.*

THAI SHRIMP OR SCALLOP CURRY Prepare Thai Green Chicken Curry as directed, except substitute 1 lb. medium shrimp in shells, peeled and deveined, or 1 lb. sea scallops for the chicken. (Thaw shrimp or scallops, if frozen. Rinse; pat dry with paper towels.) Add shrimp or scallops with the sweet pepper and eggplant.
PER SERVING *630 cal., 18 g fat (11 g sat. fat), 172 mg chol., 953 mg sodium, 85 g carb., 4 g fiber, 32 g pro.*

THAI CAULIFLOWER CURRY Prepare Thai Green Chicken Curry as directed, except substitute 4 cups cauliflower florets for the chicken.
PER SERVING *534 cal., 16 g fat (11 g sat. fat), 0 mg chol., 816 mg sodium, 89 g carb., 6 g fiber, 11 g pro.*

CHICKEN AND BROCCOLI STIR-FRY

START TO FINISH 30 minutes

½ cup cold water

2 Tbsp. soy sauce

2 Tbsp. hoisin sauce

2 tsp. cornstarch

1 tsp. grated fresh ginger

1 tsp. toasted sesame oil

1 lb. broccoli

2 Tbsp. vegetable oil

1 medium yellow sweet pepper, cut into thin bite-size strips

12 oz. skinless, boneless chicken breast halves or thighs, cut into bite-size pieces

Sesame seeds, toasted (tip, page 15) (optional)

2 cups chow mein noodles or hot cooked rice

CHOOSE YOUR FAVORITE SERVE-ALONG FOR THIS CLASSIC STIR-FRY. CRUNCHY CHOW MEIN NOODLES, WHITE OR BROWN RICE, RICE NOODLES, OR SOBA NOODLES ALL COMPLEMENT THIS DISH NICELY.

1. For sauce, in a small bowl stir together the first six ingredients (through sesame oil).

2. Cut florets from broccoli stems and separate into small pieces. Cut broccoli stems crosswise into ¼-inch slices. (Keep stem slices and florets separate.)

3. In a large skillet or wok heat 1 Tbsp. of the vegetable oil over medium-high heat. Add broccoli stems; cook and stir 1 minute. Add broccoli florets and sweet pepper; cook and stir 3 to 4 minutes or until vegetables are crisp-tender. Remove from skillet.

4. Add the remaining 1 Tbsp. vegetable oil to hot skillet. Add chicken; cook and stir 2 to 3 minutes or until no longer pink. Push chicken from center of skillet. Stir sauce; pour into center of skillet. Cook and stir until thickened and bubbly. Return vegetables to skillet; stir all ingredients together to coat with sauce. Cook 1 minute more or until heated through.

5. If desired, sprinkle stir-fry with sesame seeds. Serve over chow mein noodles and, if desired, serve with additional hoisin sauce.

MAKES 4 SERVINGS.

PER SERVING *378 cal., 16 g fat (3 g sat. fat), 49 mg chol., 877 mg sodium, 31 g carb., 6 g fiber, 29 g pro.*

PEANUT "SATAY" STIR-FRY

START TO FINISH **25 minutes**

1   14-oz. can unsweetened light coconut milk

⅓   cup peanut butter

½   tsp. salt

½   tsp. ground ginger

¼   tsp. crushed red pepper

1   lb. skinless, boneless chicken breast halves, cut into 1-inch pieces

    Salt

    Black pepper

1   Tbsp. canola oil or vegetable oil

2   cups frozen desired stir-fry vegetables

½   cup frozen peas

4   cups hot cooked ramen noodles or rice

SATAY IS AN INDONESIAN STAPLE CONSISTING OF MARINATED STRIPS OF MEAT, POULTRY, OR FISH THREADED ONTO SKEWERS, COOKED, AND SERVED WITH A SPICY PEANUT SAUCE. THIS RECIPE ADAPTS THE CONCEPT INTO A WEEKNIGHT-EASY STIR-FRY.

1. For sauce, in a bowl whisk together the first five ingredients (through crushed red pepper).
2. Sprinkle chicken lightly with additional salt and black pepper. In a large skillet or wok heat oil over medium-high heat. Add chicken; cook 6 minutes or until no longer pink. Remove from skillet.

3. Add stir-fry vegetables and peas to hot skillet. Cook and stir 2 to 3 minutes or until heated through.
4. Add sauce to mixture in skillet; return chicken. Cook and stir about 1 minute or until heated through. Serve stir-fry over ramen noodles. **MAKES 4 SERVINGS.**

PER SERVING *754 cal., 37 g fat (15 g sat. fat), 73 mg chol., 836 mg sodium, 64 g carb., 5 g fiber, 42 g pro.*

SPICY STIR-FRY TURKEY AND GREENS

START TO FINISH 30 minutes

1 Tbsp. canola oil or vegetable oil

2 medium red sweet peppers, cut into 1-inch pieces

1 small onion, cut into ½-inch-thick wedges

2 cloves garlic, minced

1 lb. ground turkey

2 to 3 tsp. curry powder

1 1-inch piece fresh ginger, grated

½ tsp. salt

½ tsp. freshly ground black pepper

6 cups fresh spinach leaves

2 to 4 Tbsp. water

1 6-oz. carton plain low-fat yogurt

4 cups hot cooked couscous

Sliced almonds, toasted (tip, page 15) (optional)

IF GROUND TURKEY ISN'T AVAILABLE, YOU CAN SWAP ANOTHER GROUND MEAT, SUCH AS CHICKEN OR LEAN GROUND PORK, IN ITS PLACE.

1. In a large skillet or wok heat oil over medium-high heat. Add sweet peppers and onion; cook and stir 3 minutes. Add garlic; cook and stir 1 minute more. Remove from skillet.

2. Add ground turkey, curry powder, ginger, salt, and black pepper to hot skillet. Cook and stir 5 minutes or until turkey is no longer pink.

3. Add spinach and the water to turkey in skillet; add vegetables. Cook and stir just until spinach is wilted. Stir in yogurt. Serve stir-fry over hot cooked couscous. If desired, sprinkle with almonds. **MAKES 4 SERVINGS.**

PER SERVING *479 cal., 19 g fat (5 g sat. fat), 91 mg chol., 426 mg sodium, 48 g carb., 5 g fiber, 29 g pro.*

MOROCCAN TURKEY PILAF

PREP 25 minutes

COOK 20 minutes

3 Tbsp. olive oil

⅓ cup finely chopped yellow onion

1 large clove garlic, minced

1 lb. uncooked ground turkey

1 28-oz. can diced tomatoes, undrained

1 cup uncooked long grain white rice

¾ cup chicken broth

1 tsp. salt

½ tsp. ground cumin

½ tsp. chili powder

½ tsp. ground cinnamon

¼ tsp. ground ginger

A COMBINATION OF WARM SPICES—INCLUDING CUMIN, CINNAMON, AND GINGER—GIVE THIS EASY-TO-MAKE RICE PILAF ITS DISTINCTIVE MOROCCAN FLAVOR.

1. In a large skillet heat oil over medium heat. Add onion and garlic; cook 5 minutes or until tender. Add turkey; cook 5 minutes more or until turkey is no longer pink. Stir in the remaining ingredients. Bring to boiling; reduce heat. Simmer, covered, 20 to 25 minutes or until rice is tender, stirring occasionally. **MAKES 4 SERVINGS.**

PER SERVING *515 cal., 25 g fat (5 g sat. fat), 89 mg chol., 1,321 mg sodium, 49 g carb., 4 g fiber, 25 g pro.*

ZESTY TURKEY SKILLET

START TO FINISH **30 minutes**

- 1 Tbsp. olive oil
- 2 turkey breast tenderloins, halved horizontally
- 1 cup salsa
- ¼ cup raisins
- 1 Tbsp. honey
- ½ tsp. ground cumin
- ¼ tsp. ground cinnamon
- 1 cup water
- ¼ tsp. salt
- ¾ cup couscous
- ¼ cup slivered almonds, toasted (tip, page 15)
- Snipped fresh Italian parsley

A FINISHING SPRINKLE OF TOASTED ALMONDS PROVIDES THIS SWEET-SPICY TURKEY SKILLET WITH A NUTTY CRUNCH.

1. In a large skillet heat oil over medium-high heat. Add turkey; cook 4 minutes or until browned, turning once. In a bowl combine salsa, raisins, honey, cumin, and cinnamon. Pour salsa mixture over turkey. Bring to boiling; reduce heat. Simmer, covered, 8 to 10 minutes or until turkey is no longer pink (165°F).

2. Meanwhile, in a medium saucepan bring the water and salt to boiling. Stir in couscous. Remove from heat. Cover and let stand 5 minutes.

3. Fluff couscous with a fork. Serve turkey and salsa mixture over couscous. Sprinkle with almonds and parsley. **MAKES 4 SERVINGS.**

PER SERVING *447 cal., 8 g fat (1 g sat. fat), 105 mg chol., 598 mg sodium, 44 g carb., 4 g fiber, 49 g pro.*

SEAFOOD

CAJUN-RUBBED SALMON

START TO FINISH 30 minutes

4 6-oz. fresh or frozen boneless salmon fillets

½ cup slivered red onion

½ cup chopped celery

2 Tbsp. snipped fresh Italian parsley

2 Tbsp. chopped dill pickle

1 Tbsp. dill pickle juice

1 Tbsp. olive oil

2 tsp. Dijon-style mustard

¼ tsp. salt

Dash sugar

2 Tbsp. Cajun Seasoning or purchased Cajun seasoning

2 Tbsp. olive oil

THE HOMEMADE CAJUN SEASONING ADDS A SPICY KICK TO THE SKILLET-SEARED SALMON. STORE THE REMAINING SEASONING— PERFECT FOR FLAVORING EVERYTHING FROM CHICKEN TO VEGGIES—IN AN AIRTIGHT CONTAINER UP TO 6 MONTHS.

1. Thaw salmon, if frozen. Preheat oven to 400°F. For relish, in a small bowl combine the next eight ingredients (through sugar). Cover and chill until ready to serve (up to 1 hour).
2. Rinse salmon; pat dry with paper towels. Sprinkle salmon with Cajun Seasoning; rub in with your fingers.
3. In a large heavy oven-going skillet heat the 2 Tbsp. oil over medium-high heat. Add salmon, skin side up; cook 2 to 3 minutes or until lightly browned. Turn salmon. Place skillet in oven. Roast until salmon flakes easily when tested with a fork. (Allow 4 to 6 minutes total per ½-inch thickness of salmon, including browning time.) Stir relish and serve with salmon. **MAKES 4 SERVINGS.**

CAJUN SEASONING In a bowl combine 2 Tbsp. packed brown sugar; 2 Tbsp. paprika; 1 Tbsp. kosher salt; 2 tsp. dried oregano, crushed; 2 tsp. dried thyme, crushed; 1 tsp. garlic powder; 1 tsp. ground cumin; ½ tsp. crushed red pepper; and ¼ tsp. cayenne pepper. Store in an airtight container at room temperature.
PER SERVING *356 cal., 21 g fat (3 g sat. fat), 94 mg chol., 778 mg sodium, 5 g carb., 1 g fiber, 34 g pro.*

SKILLET-SEARED SALMON

START TO FINISH **20 minutes**

4 5- to 6-oz. fresh or frozen
   skinless salmon fillets,
   about 1 inch thick

   Salt

   Black pepper

1 Tbsp. olive oil

4 large roma tomatoes,
   seeded and coarsely
   chopped

1 fresh jalapeño chile
   pepper, seeded and thinly
   sliced (tip, page 51)

1 Tbsp. butter

¼ cup fresh cilantro

ROMA TOMATOES HAVE FEWER SEEDS THAN OTHER TOMATO
VARIETIES AND ARE PRIZED FOR THEIR "MEATINESS". BUT WHEN
OUT OF SEASON, CHERRY TOMATOES MAY BE THE MORE
FLAVORFUL OPTION.

1. Thaw salmon, if frozen. Rinse salmon; pat dry with paper towels. Lightly sprinkle salmon with salt and pepper. In a large nonstick skillet heat olive oil over medium-high heat. Add salmon; cook 8 to 10 minutes or until salmon flakes easily when tested with a fork, turning once. If salmon browns too quickly, reduce heat to medium.

2. Add tomatoes, jalapeño, and butter to skillet; cook and stir 1 minute. Spoon over salmon; top with cilantro. **MAKES 4 SERVINGS.**

PER SERVING *339 cal., 22 g fat (5 g sat. fat), 91 mg chol., 258 mg sodium, 5 g carb., 2 g fiber, 29 g pro.*

PACIFIC NORTHWEST PAELLA

PREP 15 minutes

COOK 30 minutes

1¼ lb. fresh or frozen skinless salmon fillets, about 1 inch thick

¼ tsp. cracked black pepper

4 slices applewood–smoked bacon

3 cups sliced fresh cremini or button mushrooms (8 oz.)

1 cup chopped onion

2 cloves garlic, minced

2½ cups chicken broth

1 cup uncooked long grain white rice

2 tsp. snipped fresh thyme or ½ tsp. dried thyme, crushed

1 lb. fresh asparagus, trimmed and cut into 1-inch pieces, or one 10-oz. pkg. frozen cut asparagus, thawed

⅓ cup chopped roma tomato

PAELLA IS A SPANISH DISH THAT TYPICALLY INCLUDES A VARIETY OF MEATS AND SHELLFISH. THIS EASY-TO-MAKE VERSION FEATURES SALMON—A SPECIALTY OF THE AMERICAN PACIFIC NORTHWEST—AND APPLEWOOD–SMOKED BACON.

1. Thaw fish, if frozen. Rinse fish; pat dry with paper towels. Cut into 1-inch pieces. Season with pepper.

2. In a large deep skillet or paella pan cook bacon over medium heat until crisp. Remove bacon and drain on paper towels; reserve drippings in skillet. Crumble bacon.

3. Add mushrooms, onion, and garlic to the reserved drippings. Cook 5 minutes or until onion is tender, stirring occasionally. Stir in broth, rice, and thyme. Bring to boiling; reduce heat. Simmer, covered, 10 minutes.

4. Place fish and asparagus on top of rice mixture. Simmer, covered, 10 to 12 minutes or until fish flakes easily when tested with a fork and asparagus is crisp-tender. Sprinkle with tomato and crumbled bacon. **MAKES 6 SERVINGS.**

PER SERVING *320 cal., 10 g fat (3 g sat. fat), 56 mg chol., 569 mg sodium, 31 g carb., 2 g fiber, 27 g pro.*

SALMON PATTIES WITH PARSLEY MAYO

START TO FINISH 25 minutes

3 5-oz. pouches skinless, boneless pink salmon

½ cup panko bread crumbs

½ cup finely chopped red sweet pepper

½ cup finely chopped green onions

1 egg, lightly beaten

1 Tbsp. yellow mustard

½ cup mayonnaise

   Nonstick cooking spray

3 Tbsp. finely chopped fresh Italian parsley

1 Tbsp. lemon juice or white vinegar

1 tsp. bottled hot pepper sauce

TOPPED WITH A SPICY STIR-TOGETHER PARSLEY MAYO, THESE QUICK-TO-MAKE PATTIES TAKE ADVANTAGE OF READY-TO-USE POUCHES OF COOKED SALMON.

1. In a bowl combine the first six ingredients (through mustard) and 2 Tbsp. of the mayonnaise. Shape into eight 2½-inch patties (about ⅓ cup each).

2. Coat a very large nonstick skillet with cooking spray and heat over medium heat; add patties. Cook 4 to 5 minutes or until browned. Lightly coat patties with cooking spray; turn. Cook 4 to 5 minutes or done (160°F).

3. For parsley mayo, in a bowl stir together the remaining 2 Tbsp. mayonnaise, parsley, lemon juice, and hot sauce. Serve with salmon patties.

MAKES 4 SERVINGS.

PER SERVING *422 cal., 33 g fat (7 g sat. fat), 99 mg chol., 852 mg sodium, 8 g carb., 1 g fiber, 22 g pro.*

MAHI MAHI VERACRUZ

START TO FINISH **25 minutes**

4   6- to 8-oz. fresh or frozen
    skinless mahi mahi, red
    snapper, tilapia, or other
    fish fillets

1   Tbsp. olive oil

1   small onion, cut into thin
    wedges

1   fresh jalapeño chile
    pepper, seeded and finely
    chopped (tip, page 51)
    (optional)

1   clove garlic, minced

1   14.5-oz. can diced
    tomatoes, undrained

1   cup sliced fresh cremini or
    button mushrooms

¾   cup pimiento-stuffed
    green olives, coarsely
    chopped

1   Tbsp. snipped fresh
    oregano or ½ tsp. dried
    oregano, crushed

¼   tsp. salt

⅛   tsp. black pepper

2   cups hot cooked rice

YOU CAN CHOOSE YOUR FAMILY'S FAVORITE KIND OF FISH FOR THIS DISH. THE RULE OF THUMB FOR COOKING FISH TO THE PERFECT DONENESS IS 4 TO 6 MINUTES PER ½-INCH THICKNESS OR UNTIL FISH FLAKES EASILY WITH A FORK.

1. Thaw fish, if frozen. Rinse fish; pat dry with paper towels.
2. For sauce, in an extra-large skillet heat oil over medium heat. Add onion, jalapeño pepper (if desired), and garlic; cook 2 to 3 minutes or until onion is tender. Stir in the next six ingredients (through black pepper). Bring to boiling.

3. Gently add fish to skillet, spooning sauce over fish. Return to boiling; reduce heat. Simmer, covered, 8 to 10 minutes or until fish flakes easily when tested with a fork. If desired, using a wide spatula, carefully lift fish from skillet to a serving dish. Top with sauce; serve with rice. **MAKES 4 SERVINGS.**

PER SERVING *363 cal., 10 g fat (2 g sat. fat), 84 mg chol., 1,111 mg sodium, 31 g carb., 3 g fiber, 38 g pro.*

FISH TACOS WITH LIME SAUCE

START TO FINISH 30 minutes

- 1 lb. fresh or frozen tilapia or catfish fillets
- 3 limes
- ½ cup mayonnaise
- 1 tsp. chili powder
- ⅓ cup all-purpose flour
- ½ tsp. salt
- 2 Tbsp. vegetable oil
- 1 cup shredded cabbage
- ½ cup shredded carrot
- 1 fresh jalapeño or serrano chile pepper, thinly sliced (tip, page 51)
- 8 taco shells or 6-inch flour tortillas, warmed

THANKS TO QUICK-COOKING TILAPIA AND A SAUCE THAT DOUBLES AS A SEASONING FOR THE FISH, THESE FUN-TO-EAT TACOS CAN BE ON YOUR TABLE IN JUST A HALF-HOUR.

1. Thaw fish, if frozen. Rinse fish; pat dry with paper towels. Cut fish into 1-inch pieces.

2. For sauce, squeeze the juice from two of the limes into a bowl (about 4 Tbsp.); stir in mayonnaise and chili powder. Cut remaining lime into wedges. Transfer ⅓ cup of the sauce to a medium bowl. Add fish; toss gently to coat.

3. In a shallow dish stir together flour and salt. Add fish pieces, a few at a time; toss to coat. In a large skillet heat oil over medium heat; add fish, about one-third at a time. Cook 2 to 4 minutes or until fish flakes easily when tested with a fork, turning once. (Add more oil as necessary during cooking.) Remove with a slotted spoon and drain on paper towels.

4. Spoon fish, cabbage, carrot, and jalapeño pepper into taco shells. Serve with remaining sauce and reserved lime wedges. **MAKES 4 SERVINGS.**

PER SERVING *652 cal., 39 g fat (5 g sat. fat), 67 mg chol., 557 mg sodium, 41 g carb., 2 g fiber, 31 g pro.*

TILAPIA PASTA

START TO FINISH **40 minutes**

12 oz. fresh or frozen tilapia fillets

8 oz. dried linguine

⅛ tsp. salt

⅛ tsp. black pepper

2 Tbsp. olive oil

1 cup finely chopped onion

1 cup chopped fennel

6 cloves garlic, minced

1 Tbsp. capers

1 tsp. dried Italian seasoning, crushed

1 14.5-oz. can diced tomatoes, undrained

1 8-oz. can tomato sauce

1 Tbsp. snipped fresh Italian parsley

SWEET AND FINELY TEXTURED TILAPIA IS A DELICIOUS ADDITION TO THIS SKILLET PASTA DISH. IF IT'S NOT AVAILABLE, USE RED SNAPPER, FLOUNDER, OR GROUPER IN ITS PLACE.

1. Thaw fish, if frozen. Cook pasta according to package directions. Drain; reserve ¼ cup cooking water.

2. Meanwhile, rinse fish; pat dry with paper towels. Sprinkle with salt and pepper. In an extra-large skillet heat 1 Tbsp. of the oil over medium-high heat. Add fish; cook 6 minutes or until fish flakes easily when tested with a fork, turning once. Remove fish from skillet.

3. Add the remaining 1 Tbsp. oil to skillet. Add onion and fennel; cook 5 minutes or until tender, stirring occasionally. Stir in garlic, capers, and Italian seasoning; cook and stir 1 minute more. Stir in tomatoes, tomato sauce, and reserved pasta cooking water. Bring to boiling; reduce heat. Boil gently, uncovered, 8 minutes, stirring occasionally. Remove from heat.

4. Stir cooked pasta and fish into the sauce in skillet, stirring to break up fish slightly. Sprinkle with parsley. **MAKES 6 SERVINGS.**

PER SERVING *283 cal., 6 g fat (1 g sat. fat), 28 mg chol., 458 mg sodium, 39 g carb., 4 g fiber, 18 g pro.*

SPANISH SHRIMP STIR-FRY

START TO FINISH 35 minutes

12 oz. fresh or frozen peeled and deveined medium shrimp

2 Tbsp. vegetable oil

8 oz. small red or fingerling potatoes, cut into bite-size chunks

½ cup chicken broth

1 cup chunky salsa

4 oz. oil-cured black olives, pitted and sliced

½ tsp. smoked paprika or chili powder

4 cups hot cooked rice or couscous

Snipped fresh Italian parsley (optional)

IF YOU PREFER, SUBSTITUTE PITTED RIPE OLIVES, GREEN OLIVES, OR KALAMATA OLIVES FOR INTENSELY FLAVORED OIL-CURED BLACK OLIVES.

1. Thaw shrimp, if frozen. Rinse shrimp; pat dry with paper towels.

2. In a large skillet or wok heat oil over medium-high heat. Add potatoes; stir to coat. Cook 3 to 4 minutes or until browned, stirring frequently. Carefully add broth. Cook, covered, 8 to 10 minutes or until potatoes are tender.

3. Add shrimp to skillet. Cook and stir 3 to 4 minutes or until shrimp are opaque. Stir in salsa, olives, and paprika; heat through. Serve over hot cooked rice and, if desired, sprinkle with parsley. **MAKES 4 SERVINGS.**

PER SERVING *429 cal., 11 g fat (1 g sat. fat), 138 mg chol., 744 mg sodium, 58 g carb., 3 g fiber, 23 g pro.*

GREEK LEEKS AND SHRIMP STIR-FRY

START TO FINISH **30 minutes**

1¼ lb. fresh or frozen peeled and deveined medium shrimp

⅔ cup water

⅓ cup lemon juice

1 Tbsp. cornstarch

¾ tsp. bouquet garni seasoning or dried oregano, crushed

1 cup couscous

¼ tsp. salt

1½ cups boiling water

1 Tbsp. olive oil

1⅓ cups thinly sliced leeks

½ cup crumbled feta cheese (2 oz.)

Snipped fresh herbs (optional)

TO CLEAN THE LEEKS, CUT THEM IN HALF LENGTHWISE, THEN UNDER COOL RUNNING WATER WASH AWAY THE DIRT AND SAND TRAPPED BETWEEN THE LEAVES.

1. Thaw shrimp, if frozen. Rinse shrimp; pat dry with paper towels.

2. For sauce, in a bowl combine the ⅔ cup water, the lemon juice, cornstarch, and ¼ tsp. of the bouquet garni seasoning.

3. In another bowl combine couscous, salt, and remaining ½ tsp. bouquet garni seasoning. Stir in the 1½ cups boiling water. Cover and let stand 5 minutes.

4. Meanwhile, in an extra-large skillet or a wok heat oil over medium-high heat. Add leeks; cook and stir 2 to 3 minutes or until tender. Remove from skillet. Stir sauce; add to hot skillet. Bring to boiling. Add shrimp; cook 2 to 3 minutes or until shrimp are opaque. Return leeks to skillet; stir in ¼ cup of the cheese.

5. Fluff couscous with a fork. Serve stir-fry over couscous. Sprinkle with fresh herbs, if desired, and remaining ¼ cup cheese. **MAKES 4 SERVINGS.**

PER SERVING *433 cal., 10 g fat (4 g sat. fat), 232 mg chol., 548 mg sodium, 45 g carb., 3 g fiber, 38 g pro.*

CUMIN-LIME SHRIMP ON JICAMA RICE

START TO FINISH **30 minutes**

- 12 oz. fresh or frozen peeled and deveined medium shrimp
- 3 tsp. olive oil
- 1½ cups chopped yellow onions
- 1 medium fresh Anaheim chile pepper, seeded and sliced (tip, page 51)
- 1½ Tbsp. chili powder
- 1½ tsp. ground cumin
- 1 cup hot cooked brown rice
- 1½ cups peeled jicama cut into thin bite-size strips
- 2 Tbsp. lime juice
- 2 Tbsp. 60% to 70% vegetable oil spread
- ¼ tsp. salt
- ⅓ cup snipped fresh cilantro
- Lime wedges (optional)

JICAMA ADDS A SLIGHTLY SWEET, CRUNCHY ELEMENT TO THE BROWN RICE. WHEN BUYING THIS MEXICAN ROOT VEGETABLE, CHOOSE ONE THAT IS FIRM WITH SMOOTH, UNBLEMISHED SKIN. KEEP IN MIND THAT SMALLER JICAMA ROOTS HAVE A SWEETER, MORE APPEALING FLAVOR THAN LARGER ONES.

1. Thaw shrimp, if frozen. Rinse shrimp; pat dry with paper towels. In a large nonstick skillet heat 1 tsp. of the oil over medium-high heat. Tilt and swirl skillet to coat. Add onions and chile pepper; cook 3 minutes or until tender, stirring frequently. Stir in shrimp, chili powder, and cumin; cook 3 to 4 minutes or until shrimp are opaque.

2. Meanwhile, spoon hot cooked rice into a serving bowl; stir in jicama. Cover and let stand until ready to serve.

3. Remove skillet from heat; stir in remaining 2 tsp. oil, the lime juice, vegetable oil spread, and salt. Cover and let stand 5 minutes.

4. Stir cilantro into rice. Serve shrimp over rice. If desired, serve with lime wedges. **MAKES 4 SERVINGS.**

PER SERVING *284 cal., 11 g fat (2 g sat. fat), 129 mg chol., 350 mg sodium, 26 g carb., 6 g fiber, 21 g pro.*

LEMON-GARLIC SHRIMP AND PASTA

START TO FINISH 25 minutes

- 12 oz. fresh or frozen peeled and deveined medium shrimp
- 1 lemon
- 8 oz. dried fettucine
- 2 Tbsp. olive oil
- 3 to 4 cloves garlic, thinly sliced
- 6 cups fresh baby spinach
- ½ tsp. dried Italian seasoning, crushed
- Salt
- Black pepper
- Fresh dill sprigs (optional)

SIX CUPS OF BABY SPINACH MAY SEEM LIKE A LOT, BUT ONCE IT GOES INTO THE SKILLET IT WILL WILT DOWN TO LESS THAN ONE CUP. FOR A PEPPERY BITE, REPLACE HALF OF THE SPINACH WITH BABY ARUGULA.

1. Thaw shrimp, if frozen. Rinse shrimp; pat dry with paper towels. Remove 1 tsp. zest and squeeze 2 Tbsp. juice from lemon. In a large Dutch oven cook pasta according to package directions; drain.

2. Meanwhile, in an extra-large skillet heat oil over medium heat. Add garlic; cook and stir 1 minute. Add shrimp; cook 3 to 4 minutes or until shrimp are opaque, turning frequently. Add spinach and cooked pasta; toss just until spinach begins to wilt. Stir in reserved lemon zest and juice and the Italian seasoning. Season to taste with salt and pepper. If desired, top with fresh dill. **MAKES 4 SERVINGS.**

PER SERVING *359 cal., 9 g fat (1 g sat. fat), 107 mg chol., 696 mg sodium, 50 g carb., 5 g fiber, 21 g pro.*

SHRIMP, MANGO, AND COUSCOUS SKILLET

START TO FINISH **35 minutes**

1½ lb. fresh or frozen medium shrimp in shells

4 tsp. olive oil

1 cup Israeli (large pearl) couscous

1¼ cups water

¼ cup bottled mango chipotle salad dressing

¼ tsp. salt

¼ tsp. black pepper

1½ cups chopped fresh or refrigerated mango

½ cup crumbled queso fresco (2 oz.)

Snipped fresh Italian parsley

ISRAELI COUSCOUS IS A SMALL ROUND TYPE OF PASTA THAT IS LARGER THAN THE GRANULAR REGULAR COUSCOUS. IF IT'S NOT AVAILABLE, SUBSTITUTE RICE-SHAPE ORZO PASTA.

1. Thaw shrimp, if frozen. Peel and devein shrimp, leaving tails intact, if desired. Rinse shrimp; pat dry with paper towels. In a medium saucepan heat 2 tsp. of the oil over medium-high heat. Add couscous; cook and stir 3 to 4 minutes or until lightly browned. Add the water. Bring to boiling; reduce heat. Simmer, covered, 8 to 10 minutes or until couscous is tender. Remove from heat.

2. In an extra-large nonstick skillet heat the remaining 2 tsp. oil over medium-high heat. Add shrimp; cook and stir 3 minutes or until shrimp are opaque. Stir in cooked couscous, salad dressing, salt, and pepper. Cook and stir 2 to 3 minutes more or until heated through. Stir in mango. Sprinkle with queso fresco and parsley. **MAKES 5 SERVINGS.**

PER SERVING *348 cal., 11 g fat (3 g sat. fat), 198 mg chol., 529 mg sodium, 34 g carb., 2 g fiber, 29 g pro.*

SPEEDY PAELLA

START TO FINISH 20 minutes

8 oz. fresh or frozen sea scallops

8 oz. fresh or frozen peeled and deveined cooked shrimp

1 10-oz. pkg. frozen long grain white rice with vegetables (peas, corn, and carrots)

½ to 1 tsp. ground turmeric

1 Tbsp. canola oil

1⅓ cups coarsely chopped roma tomatoes (4 medium)

Salt

Black pepper

Snipped fresh Italian parsley (optional)

A PACKAGE OF FROZEN PRECOOKED RICE AND VEGGIES KEEPS THE INGREDIENTS LIST SHORT AND MAKES THIS SPANISH-STYLE SKILLET SUPER QUICK AND EASY TO PREPARE.

1. Thaw scallops and shrimp, if frozen. Rinse scallops and shrimp; pat dry with paper towels. Cut any large scallops in half. Prepare rice according to microwave package directions. Stir in turmeric.

2. Meanwhile, in a large skillet heat oil over medium heat. Add scallops; cook 3 minutes or until scallops are opaque, turning once. Stir in cooked shrimp and chopped tomatoes; heat through.

3. Add hot rice to seafood mixture in skillet; toss gently to combine. Season to taste with salt and pepper. If desired, sprinkle with parsley.

MAKES 4 SERVINGS.

PER SERVING *229 cal., 5 g fat (1 g sat. fat), 129 mg chol., 374 mg sodium, 22 g carb., 2 g fiber, 24 g pro.*

SPANISH SHRIMP AND SCALLOP SAUTÉ

START TO FINISH **25 minutes**

16 fresh or frozen medium shrimp in shells (8 oz.)

8 fresh or frozen sea scallops (8 oz.)

1 Tbsp. all-purpose flour

2 tsp. smoked paprika

½ tsp. salt

¼ tsp. black pepper

⅛ to ¼ tsp. cayenne pepper

2 Tbsp. butter

6 cloves garlic, thinly sliced

1 cup grape or cherry tomatoes, halved

¼ cup reduced-sodium chicken broth

3 Tbsp. dry vermouth or white wine

1 Tbsp. lemon juice

3 Tbsp. finely snipped fresh Italian parsley

3 Tbsp. snipped fresh chives

2 cups hot cooked brown rice

THIS SEAFOOD SKILLET PAIRS WELL WITH BROWN RICE, BUT YOU CAN CHOOSE ANOTHER SERVE-ALONG IF YOU PREFER. PASTA, WHITE RICE, OR CRUSTY BREAD ARE DELICIOUS OPTIONS.

1. Thaw shrimp and scallops, if frozen. Peel and devein shrimp, leaving tails intact if desired. Halve scallops horizontally. Rinse shrimp and scallops; pat dry with paper towels.

2. In a resealable plastic bag combine flour, paprika, ¼ tsp. of the salt, the black pepper, and cayenne pepper. Add shrimp and scallops; seal bag and shake to coat.

3. In a large nonstick skillet melt 1 Tbsp. of the butter over medium-high heat. Add garlic and the remaining ¼ tsp. salt; cook and stir 30 seconds. Add shrimp and scallops in an even layer; cook 2 minutes. Stir in tomatoes, broth, vermouth, and lemon juice. Cook 2 to 3 minutes more or until shrimp and scallops are opaque, stirring occasionally. Remove from heat.

4. Stir in the remaining 1 Tbsp. butter, the parsley, and chives. Serve with brown rice.

MAKES 4 SERVINGS.

PER SERVING *276 cal., 7 g fat (4 g sat. fat), 97 mg chol., 659 mg sodium, 31 g carb., 3 g fiber, 19 g pro.*

CRAB CAKES 4 WAYS

PREP 30 minutes

COOK 12 minutes CHILL 2 hours

- ¼ cup finely chopped red sweet pepper
- 2 Tbsp. chopped green onion
- 1 clove garlic, minced
- 2 Tbsp. butter
- 1 lb. cooked lump crabmeat, drained
- ⅓ cup mayonnaise
- ⅔ cup fine dry bread crumbs
- 2 Tbsp. snipped fresh Italian parsley
- 2 tsp. Dijon-style mustard
- 2 Tbsp. olive oil

ALLOWING THE CRAB CAKE PATTIES TO CHILL FOR A FEW HOURS IN THE REFRIGERATOR BEFORE PAN-FRYING THEM PREVENTS THEM FROM FALLING APART IN THE SKILLET.

1. Line a baking sheet with parchment paper. In a small skillet cook sweet pepper, green onion, and garlic in hot butter 4 minutes or until tender. Transfer to a medium bowl and let cool slightly.
2. Stir crabmeat, mayonnaise, ⅓ cup of the bread crumbs, the parsley, and mustard into the sweet pepper mixture. Shape crabmeat mixture into eight patties and place on the prepared baking sheet.
3. Place remaining bread crumbs in a shallow dish. Dip each patty into bread crumbs; return to baking sheet. Cover loosely and chill patties 2 to 4 hours.
4. In a large skillet heat oil over medium heat. Cook crab cakes, half at a time, 3 minutes on each side or until golden brown and heated through. (Keep cooked crab cakes warm in a 200°F oven while cooking remaining crab cakes.) **MAKES 4 SERVINGS.**
MEXICAN CRAB CAKES Prepare as directed, except reduce red sweet pepper to 2 Tbsp. and cook 1 fresh jalapeño pepper, seeded and minced, with the mixture in Step 1. Substitute snipped fresh cilantro for the parsley, and add 1½ tsp. each chili powder and ground cumin to the mixture in Step 2.

RED CURRY-BASIL CRAB CAKES Prepare as directed, except substitute fresh snipped basil for the parsley and add 1½ Tbsp. red curry paste to the mixture in Step 2. If desired, serve with lime wedges and top with fresh cilantro.
CAJUN CRAB CAKES Prepare as directed, except reduce sweet red pepper to 2 Tbsp. and cook 2 Tbsp. finely chopped celery with the mixture in Step 1. Add 1 tsp. Cajun seasoning to the mixture in Step 2. If desired, serve with cajun mayonnaise or tartar sauce and lemon wedges.
PESTO CRAB CAKES Prepare as directed, except reduce mayonnaise to 3 Tbsp., omit parsley, and add 2 Tbsp. basil pesto to the mixture in Step 2. Serve crab cakes with additional basil pesto, 2 Tbsp. grated Parmesan cheese, and 1 Tbsp. snipped fresh basil.
PER SERVING 448 cal., 29 g fat (7 g sat. fat), 143 mg chol., 796 mg sodium, 15 g carb., 1 g fiber, 30 g pro.

BEER-STEAMED MUSSELS WITH SAUSAGE AND FENNEL

START TO FINISH 35 minutes

- 2 lb. fresh black mussels, scrubbed, rinsed, and beards removed
- 9 qt. water
- 9 Tbsp. salt
- 2 tsp. olive oil
- 4 oz. uncooked hot Italian turkey sausage link, casing removed
- 6 cloves garlic, thinly sliced
- 1 cup onion, chopped
- ½ cup thinly sliced fennel
- 1 tsp. fennel seeds
- ½ tsp. salt
- ½ tsp. crushed red pepper
- 1 cup seeded and chopped tomatoes
- 1 12-oz. bottle mild beer
- 1 cup reduced-sodium chicken broth
- 1 lemon, cut into 6 wedges
- ⅓ cup snipped fresh Italian parsley
  Sliced crusty bread (optional)
  Lemon wedges (optional)

WHEN BUYING MUSSELS, THEY SHOULD HAVE TIGHTLY CLOSED SHELLS OR CLOSE QUICKLY WHEN TAPPED. AVOID MUSSELS WITH OPEN, BROKEN, OR LOOSELY CLAMPED SHELLS.

1. Scrub mussels under cold running water. Using your fingers, pull out any beards visible between mussel shells; discard. In an extra-large bowl combine 3 qt. of the water and 3 Tbsp. of the salt. Add mussels; soak 15 minutes. Drain and rinse thoroughly; drain. Repeat two more times with fresh water and salt. Drain and rinse mussels thoroughly.

2. In an extra-large skillet with a tight-fitting lid heat oil over medium heat. Add sausage; cook until browned. Remove sausage and drain on paper towels; reserve drippings in skillet.

3. Add garlic to skillet; cook and stir over medium heat 1 to 2 minutes or just until golden. Stir in the next five ingredients (through crushed red pepper). Cook, covered, 5 minutes or until vegetables are tender. Stir in tomatoes and cooked sausage.

4. Increase heat to high. Add beer and broth to skillet; bring to boiling. Stir in mussels and the six lemon wedges. Cook, covered, 2 to 3 minutes or just until mussels open. Discard any mussels that do not open. Sprinkle with parsley. Serve mussels in bowls with broth mixture and, if desired, crusty bread and additional lemon wedges. **MAKES 6 SERVINGS.**

PER SERVING *230 cal., 7 g fat (1 g sat. fat), 55 mg chol., 854 mg sodium, 15 g carb., 2 g fiber, 23 g pro.*

VEGETARIAN

TOMATO, GREENS, AND CHICKPEA SKILLET

START TO FINISH **25 minutes**

3   Tbsp. olive oil

½   cup chopped onion

1   clove garlic, minced

1   Tbsp. curry powder

1   14.5-oz. can diced tomatoes, undrained

¼   tsp. salt

1   15-oz. can garbanzo beans (chickpeas), rinsed and drained

2   cups torn fresh Swiss chard or spinach

4   eggs

Salt

Black pepper

Fresh cilantro sprigs (optional)

SERVE THIS CURRIED VEGETABLE-AND-EGG DISH WITH CRUSTY BREAD, PITA WEDGES, OR POLENTA.

1. In a large skillet heat 2 Tbsp. of the oil over medium heat. Add onion and garlic; cook and stir 5 minutes. Add curry powder; cook and stir 1 minute. Add tomatoes and salt; cook 3 minutes, stirring occasionally. Add chickpeas; cook and stir 3 minutes or until heated through. Add Swiss chard; cook and stir 3 minutes or until slightly wilted.

2. Meanwhile, in another large skillet heat the remaining 1 Tbsp. oil over medium heat. Break eggs into skillet. Sprinkle with salt and pepper. Reduce heat to low. Cook, covered, 3 to 4 minutes or until whites are completely set and yolks start to thicken.

3. Serve cooked eggs with tomato mixture. If desired, top with cilantro. **MAKES 4 SERVINGS.**
PER SERVING *279 cal., 17 g fat (3 g sat. fat), 186 mg chol., 675 mg sodium, 21 g carb., 2 g fiber, 12 g pro.*

BLACK BEAN CAKES WITH SALSA

START TO FINISH 25 minutes

1½ cups salsa

2 15-oz. cans black beans, rinsed and drained

1 8.5-oz. pkg. corn muffin mix

1 egg, lightly beaten

1 medium fresh jalapeño chile pepper, seeded and finely chopped (tip, page 51)

2½ tsp. chili powder

2 Tbsp. olive oil

½ cup sour cream

½ tsp. chili powder

CORN MUFFIN MIX GIVES THESE BEAN PATTIES A SUBTLE SWEETNESS THAT IS BALANCED PERFECTLY WITH SPICY JALAPEÑO CHILE PEPPER AND TANGY SALSA.

1. Drain ½ cup of the salsa in a colander. In a large bowl mash black beans with a potato masher or fork. Stir in the drained salsa, muffin mix, egg, half of the jalapeño pepper, and the 2½ tsp. chili powder.

2. In an extra-large skillet heat 1 Tbsp. of the oil over medium-high heat. Drop four ⅓-cup mounds of bean mixture into hot skillet. Using a spatula, flatten mounds into 3½-inch cakes. Cook 6 minutes or until browned, turning once. Remove from skillet. Repeat with remaining oil and bean mixture.

3. In a bowl combine sour cream and the ½ tsp. chili powder. Top bean cakes with the remaining salsa and jalapeño pepper. Serve with sour cream. **MAKES 4 SERVINGS.**

PER SERVING *532 cal., 16 g fat (4 g sat. fat), 59 mg chol., 1,625 mg sodium, 85 g carb., 12 g fiber, 19 g pro.*

PASTA, RED BEAN, AND PARSLEY TOSS

START TO FINISH **30 minutes**

8 oz. dried medium shell pasta or desired pasta

3 cups broccoli florets

1 15-oz. can red beans, undrained

1 Tbsp. olive oil

1½ cups chopped onions

½ tsp. salt

½ cup vegetable broth

1½ tsp. chili powder

½ cup finely shredded Parmesan cheese (2 oz.)

¼ cup snipped fresh Italian parsley

Shaved Parmesan cheese (optional)

WHEN ADDED AT THE END OF COOKING, ITALIAN PARSLEY PROVIDES A SPARK OF FRESH FLAVOR TO THIS PASTA-BEAN SKILLET.

1. Cook pasta according to package directions, adding broccoli the last 3 minutes of cooking; drain. Set aside.

2. Meanwhile, drain beans, reserving ¼ cup of the liquid. In an extra-large skillet heat oil over medium-high heat. Add onions and salt; reduce heat to medium. Cook 5 minutes or until onions are tender, stirring occasionally.

3. Increase heat to high; stir in cooked pasta mixture, beans, the reserved bean liquid, broth, and chili powder. Cook 2 minutes, stirring occasionally. Add shredded cheese and parsley. Cook and stir until cheese is melted. If desired, top with shaved cheese. **MAKES 4 SERVINGS.**

PER SERVING *422 cal., 8 g fat (3 g sat. fat), 11 mg chol., 796 mg sodium, 70 g carb., 11 g fiber, 19 g pro.*

BRUSSELS SPROUTS AND NOODLE STIR-FRY WITH CILANTRO AND ALMONDS

START TO FINISH **30 minutes**

- 3 oz. dried thin whole wheat spaghetti
- 2 Tbsp. olive oil
- 1 cup thinly sliced red onion
- 3 cloves garlic, minced
- 12 oz. fresh Brussels sprouts, trimmed and thinly sliced
- 1 Tbsp. grated fresh ginger
- ¼ to ½ tsp. crushed red pepper
- ½ cup reduced-sodium vegetable broth
- 2 Tbsp. reduced-sodium soy sauce
- ½ cup shredded carrot
- ⅓ cup snipped fresh cilantro
- 3 Tbsp. slivered almonds, toasted (tip, page 15)

SAVE TIME THINLY SLICING THE BRUSSELS SPROUTS BY USING THE SLICING ATTACHMENT ON A FOOD PROCESSOR. OR LOOK FOR SHREDDED FRESH BRUSSELS SPROUTS WITH THE PACKAGED SALAD MIXES IN YOUR SUPERMARKET.

1. Break spaghetti into 1-inch pieces. Cook spaghetti according to package directions; drain. Return spaghetti to hot pan; cover and keep warm.

2. In a large skillet or wok heat oil over medium-high heat. Add onion and garlic; cook and stir 1 minute. Add Brussels sprouts, ginger, and crushed red pepper; cook and stir 1 minute. Add broth and soy sauce. Cook 2 minutes more or until liquid is nearly evaporated, stirring occasionally. Remove from heat.

3. Stir in cooked spaghetti, carrot, and cilantro. Sprinkle with almonds. **MAKES 4 SERVINGS.**

PER SERVING *230 cal., 10 g fat (2 g sat. fat), 392 mg sodium, 30 g carb., 6 g fiber, 8 g pro.*

GINGERED VEGETABLE-TOFU STIR-FRY

¾ cup water

¼ cup dry sherry, dry white wine, or vegetable broth

3 Tbsp. soy sauce

1 Tbsp. cornstarch

½ tsp. sugar

1 Tbsp. olive oil

2 tsp. grated fresh ginger

1 lb. fresh asparagus, cut into 1-inch pieces, or one 10-oz. pkg. frozen cut asparagus, thawed and well drained

1 small yellow summer squash, halved lengthwise and sliced

¼ cup sliced green onions

12 oz. extra-firm tofu, cut into ½-inch cubes and patted dry

½ cup chopped toasted almonds (tip, page 15)

2 cups hot cooked brown rice

PAT THE TOFU CUBES DRY USING PAPER TOWELS BEFORE ADDING THEM TO THE SKILLET. THIS WILL HELP THE TOFU BROWN AND PREVENT IT FROM STICKING TO THE SKILLET.

1. For sauce, in a bowl stir together the first five ingredients (through sugar).

2. In a large skillet or wok heat oil over medium-high heat. (Add more oil as needed during cooking.) Add ginger; cook and stir 15 seconds. Add fresh asparagus (if using) and squash; cook and stir 3 minutes. Add thawed asparagus (if using) and green onions; cook and stir 2 minutes more or until asparagus is crisp-tender. Remove vegetables from skillet.

3. Add tofu to skillet. Carefully cook and stir over medium-high heat 2 to 3 minutes or until tofu is lightly browned. Remove from skillet. Stir sauce; add to skillet. Cook and stir until thickened and bubbly. Return cooked vegetables and tofu to skillet. Stir all ingredients into sauce to coat. Cook, covered, 1 minute more or until heated through. Stir in almonds. Serve stir-fry over rice. **MAKES 4 SERVINGS.**

PER SERVING *329 cal., 13 g fat (1 g sat. fat), 836 mg sodium, 37 g carb., 6 g fiber, 15 g pro.*

TOFU PAD THAI

START TO FINISH **35 minutes**

5 oz. dried brown rice fettuccine

3 Tbsp. packed brown sugar

3 Tbsp. rice vinegar

2 Tbsp. Asian chile bean sauce

2 Tbsp. reduced-sodium soy sauce or fish sauce

1 Tbsp. tamarind pulp concentrate*

3 cloves garlic, minced

Nonstick cooking spray

1 egg, lightly beaten (optional)

1 Tbsp. vegetable oil

3 cups coarsely shredded napa cabbage

1 cup julienne carrots

4 green onions, cut into 1-inch pieces

½ to 1 fresh Thai chile pepper, cut into thin strips (tip, page 51)

1 18-oz. pkg. firm tub-style tofu, drained and cut into ½-inch slices

¼ cup unsalted dry-roasted peanuts, chopped

2 Tbsp. snipped fresh cilantro

1 lime, quartered

IF YOUR REGULAR SUPERMARKET DOESN'T HAVE AN EXPANSIVE ASIAN SECTION, HEAD TO AN ASIAN FOOD STORE FOR CHILE BEAN SAUCE, TAMARIND PULP CONCENTRATE, AND FRESH THAI CHILE PEPPERS.

1. Cook fettuccine according to package directions, except cook 2 minutes less than the suggested time; drain. Rinse with cold water; drain again.

2. Meanwhile, for sauce, in a bowl combine the next six ingredients (through garlic).

3. Coat a large nonstick skillet or wok with cooking spray; heat over medium heat. Add egg, if using. Immediately begin stirring gently but continuously until egg resembles small pieces of cooked egg surrounded by liquid egg. Stop stirring; cook 20 to 30 seconds or until egg is set. Turn egg over; cook 20 to 30 seconds more or until egg is cooked through. Transfer egg to a cutting board; set aside.

4. Add 1 tsp. of the oil to skillet; add cabbage, carrots, green onions, and chile pepper. Cook and stir over medium-high heat 2 to 3 minutes or until vegetables are crisp-tender. Remove vegetables from skillet.

5. Add the remaining 2 tsp. oil to skillet; add tofu. Cook 4 to 5 minutes or until tofu is lightly browned, turning occasionally. Remove tofu from skillet. Add fettuccine and sauce. Cook and stir 2 to 3 minutes or until fettuccine is tender but still firm. Return vegetables and tofu to skillet. Cook 1 to 2 minutes or until heated through, gently stirring occasionally (tofu will slightly break apart). Cut egg into thin slices; gently stir into fettuccine mixture. Sprinkle servings with peanuts and cilantro, and serve with lime quarters. **MAKES 4 SERVINGS.**

*Tip Or substitute 1½ tsp. each lime juice and brown sugar.

PER SERVING *393 cal., 14 g fat (2 g sat. fat), 568 mg sodium, 51 g carb., 4 g fiber, 16 g pro.*

FARFALLE WITH MUSHROOMS AND SPINACH

START TO FINISH **20 minutes**

5½ cups dried farfalle (bow-tie pasta) (12 oz.)

2 Tbsp. olive oil

1 cup chopped onion

2 cups sliced portobello or other fresh mushrooms

4 cloves garlic, minced

8 cups fresh baby spinach

2 tsp. snipped fresh thyme

¼ tsp. black pepper

¼ cup shredded Parmesan cheese

IF GOOD-LOOKING FRESH PORTOBELLO MUSHROOMS ARE NOT AVAILABLE, YOU CAN USE CREMINI MUSHROOMS IN THEIR PLACE. THESE SMALLER MUSHROOMS ARE THE LESS MATURE FORM OF THE PORTOBELLO MUSHROOM AND HAVE A SLIGHTLY LESS INTENSE FLAVOR.

1. Cook farfalle according to package directions; drain.

2. Meanwhile, in an extra-large skillet heat oil over medium heat. Add onion, mushrooms, and garlic; cook and stir 2 to 3 minutes or until mushrooms are nearly tender. Stir in spinach, thyme, and pepper; cook 1 minute or until heated through and spinach is slightly wilted. Stir in cooked pasta; toss gently to mix. Sprinkle with cheese. **MAKES 4 SERVINGS.**

PER SERVING *451 cal., 11 g fat (2 g sat. fat), 4 mg chol., 131 mg sodium, 74 g carb., 5 g fiber, 17 g pro.*

SKILLET BUCATINI WITH SPRING VEGETABLES

START TO FINISH 35 minutes

4 oz. dried bucatini, thick spaghetti, or regular spaghetti

2 Tbsp. peanut oil or vegetable oil

12 oz. asparagus spears, trimmed and cut into 2-inch pieces (2½ cups)

6 cloves garlic, sliced

3 cups red and yellow cherry tomatoes, halved

¾ tsp. salt

¾ cup snipped fresh basil

½ cup sliced pitted Kalamata olives

¼ tsp. freshly ground black pepper

½ cup grated Parmesan cheese

Lemon wedges (optional)

BUCATINI IS A LONG, HOLLOW PASTA, SLIGHTLY THICKER THAN SPAGHETTI. IF YOU CAN'T FIND IT, SUBSTITUTE ANY OTHER VARIETY OF LONG PASTA.

1. In a large Dutch oven cook pasta according to package directions. Drain, reserving ½ cup of the cooking water. Return pasta to hot pan. Drizzle with 1 Tbsp. of the oil; toss gently to coat.
2. Heat an extra-large skillet over high heat. Add the remaining 1 Tbsp. oil.
3. Add asparagus; cook and stir 2 minutes or until bright green. Add garlic; cook and stir 10 seconds or until fragrant. Add cherry tomatoes and ½ tsp. of the salt; cook and stir 30 seconds. Add basil and olives; cook and stir 30 seconds more. Remove from heat.

4. Gently stir in cooked pasta, the remaining ¼ tsp. salt, and the pepper. Stir in enough of the reserved pasta cooking water to reach desired consistency. Sprinkle with cheese and, if desired, serve with lemon wedges. **MAKES 4 SERVINGS.**

PER SERVING *278 cal., 13 g fat (3 g sat. fat), 9 mg chol., 785 mg sodium, 33 g carb., 5 g fiber, 11 g pro.*

VEGGIE-STUFFED PASTA SHELLS

START TO FINISH 40 minutes

12   dried jumbo shell
      macaroni

1½   cups shredded carrots

1⅓   cups shredded zucchini

½   cup finely chopped onion

1   Tbsp. olive oil

1   10-oz. pkg. frozen
      chopped spinach, thawed
      and well drained

½   of a 15-oz. carton ricotta
      cheese (about 1 cup)

1½   cups shredded Italian-
      blend cheeses (6 oz.)

¼   tsp. salt

1   24-oz. jar pasta sauce

BE SURE TO SQUEEZE OUT ALL THE EXCESS MOISTURE FROM THE THAWED FROZEN SPINACH TO PREVENT THE FILLING FROM BECOMING WATERY.

1. In a large saucepan cook pasta according to package directions; drain. Rinse pasta with cold water; drain again.

2. Meanwhile, in a large skillet cook carrots, zucchini, and onion in hot oil over medium-high heat 3 to 5 minutes or until tender. Stir in spinach; cook and stir 1 minute. Transfer spinach mixture to a large bowl.

3. Stir ricotta cheese, 1 cup of the shredded cheese, and salt into vegetable mixture. Spoon a rounded 2 Tbsp. filling into each pasta shell. Pour pasta sauce into skillet; place filled shells on sauce. Heat shells and sauce, covered, over medium heat 10 minutes or until heated through. Sprinkle with remaining shredded cheese. **MAKES 4 SERVINGS.**

PER SERVING *471 cal., 22 g fat (11 g sat. fat), 57 mg chol., 1,219 mg sodium, 44 g carb., 8 g fiber, 25 g pro.*

WILD MUSHROOM RAVIOLI SKILLET LASAGNA

START TO FINISH **25 minutes**

- 1 egg, lightly beaten
- ½ of a 15-oz. carton fat-free ricotta cheese
- 2 Tbsp. grated Romano or Parmesan cheese
- 2 cups lower sodium pasta sauce with basil
- ¾ cup water
- 2 8- to 9-oz. pkg. refrigerated wild mushroom-filled ravioli or agnolotti
- 2 cups chopped fresh kale

TO CUT DOWN ON PREP TIME, PURCHASE PREWASHED AND CHOPPED KALE TO USE IN THIS SKILLET LASAGNA. IF YOU PREFER, YOU CAN SWAP OUT THE KALE FOR ANOTHER GREEN, SUCH AS SWISS CHARD OR SPINACH.

1. In a bowl combine egg, ricotta cheese, and Romano cheese.

2. In a large skillet combine pasta sauce and the water. Bring to boiling. Stir in ravioli and kale. Return to boiling; reduce heat. Spoon ricotta mixture into large mounds on top of ravioli mixture.

3. Simmer, covered, 10 minutes or until ricotta mixture is set and ravioli is tender but still firm.

MAKES 4 SERVINGS.

PER SERVING *416 cal., 16 g fat (7 g sat. fat), 118 mg chol., 975 mg sodium, 45 g carb., 4 g fiber, 26 g pro.*

EGGPLANT PARMIGIANA

START TO FINISH 30 minutes

1 small eggplant (12 oz.)

1 egg, lightly beaten

1 Tbsp. water

¼ cup all-purpose flour

2 Tbsp. vegetable oil

⅓ cup grated Parmesan cheese

1 cup meatless spaghetti sauce

¾ cup shredded mozzarella cheese (3 oz.)

Shredded fresh basil (optional)

EGGPLANT IS THE STAR OF THIS DISH, SO BE SURE TO CHOOSE A QUALITY ONE. IT SHOULD BE FIRM, SMOOTH-SKINNED, AND HEAVY FOR ITS SIZE.

1. Wash and peel eggplant; cut crosswise into ½-inch slices. In a shallow bowl combine egg and the water. Place the flour in a second shallow bowl. Dip eggplant slices into egg mixture, then into flour, turning to coat both sides.

2. In a large skillet cook eggplant, half at a time, in hot oil over medium-high heat 4 to 6 minutes or until golden, turning once. (If eggplant browns too quickly, add additional oil and reduce heat to medium.) Drain on paper towels.

3. Wipe the skillet with paper towels. Arrange the cooked eggplant slices in the skillet; sprinkle with the Parmesan cheese. Top with spaghetti sauce and mozzarella cheese. Cook, covered, over medium-low heat 5 to 7 minutes or until heated through. If desired, top with basil. **MAKES 4 SERVINGS.**

PER SERVING *250 cal., 15 g fat (5 g sat. fat), 70 mg chol., 563 mg sodium, 20 g carb., 5 g fiber, 12 g pro.*

SMOKY MUSHROOM STROGANOFF

START TO FINISH 25 minutes

1 8.8-oz. pkg. dried pappardelle (wide egg noodles)

1 Tbsp. olive oil

1½ lb. sliced mushrooms, such as button, cremini, and/or shiitake

2 cloves garlic, minced

1 8-oz. carton light sour cream

2 Tbsp. all-purpose flour

1½ tsp. smoked paprika

¼ tsp. black pepper

1 cup vegetable broth

Snipped fresh Italian parsley (optional)

KEEP IN MIND THAT WILD MUSHROOMS, SUCH AS CREMINI OR SHIITAKE MUSHROOMS, WILL ADD A MORE INTENSE FLAVOR TO THE SAUCE THAN BUTTON MUSHROOMS.

1. Cook noodles according to package directions. Drain; keep warm.

2. In an extra-large skillet heat oil over medium-high heat. Add mushrooms and garlic to hot oil; cook 5 to 8 minutes or until tender, stirring occasionally. (Reduce heat if mushrooms brown too quickly.) Transfer mushrooms to a bowl; cover and keep warm.

3. For sauce, in a medium bowl stir together sour cream, flour, smoked paprika, and pepper. Add broth, stirring until smooth; add to skillet. Cook and stir until thickened and bubbly; cook and stir 1 minute more. Serve sauce and mushrooms over noodles. If desired, sprinkle with parsley. **MAKES 4 SERVINGS.**

PER SERVING *407 cal., 13 g fat (5 g sat. fat), 72 mg chol., 443 mg sodium, 59 g carb., 4 g fiber, 17 g pro.*

SKILLET VEGETABLES ON CHEESE TOASTS

START TO FINISH 25 minutes

- 2 Tbsp. olive oil
- 8 fresh button mushrooms, halved
- ½ of an 8-oz. pkg. peeled fresh baby carrots, halved lengthwise
- 1 small red onion, cut into thin wedges
- 4 cloves garlic, coarsely chopped
- 2 Tbsp. water
  Salt
  Black pepper
- 8 slices hearty whole grain bread
- 4 oz. soft goat cheese (chèvre)
  Fresh basil (optional)

SOFT GOAT CHEESE PROVIDES A CREAMY BUT TANGY BASE FOR THE SAUTÉED VEGGIES. IF YOU PREFER, YOU CAN USE SOFTENED CREAM CHEESE OR RICOTTA CHEESE IN ITS PLACE.

1. Preheat broiler. In a large skillet heat the 2 Tbsp. oil over medium-high heat. Add mushrooms, carrots, onion, and garlic; cook and stir 2 to 3 minutes or just until vegetables begin to brown. Add the water; reduce heat to medium. Cook, covered, 5 minutes or until vegetables are crisp-tender, stirring once. Sprinkle with salt and pepper.

2. Meanwhile, for cheese toasts, place bread slices on a baking sheet. Broil about 3 inches from the heat 1 to 2 minutes or until lightly toasted. Spread with goat cheese. Broil 1 to 2 minutes more or until cheese is softened.

3. Spoon vegetables on top of cheese toasts. If desired, drizzle with additional oil and/or sprinkle with basil. **MAKES 4 SERVINGS.**

PER SERVING *461 cal., 21 g fat (6 g sat. fat), 13 mg chol., 596 mg sodium, 56 g carb., 8 g fiber, 15 g pro.*

SKILLET-ROASTED CAULIFLOWER STEAKS WITH JALAPEÑO CREAMED SPINACH

PREP 30 minutes

ROAST 15 minutes at 375°F

- 1 to 2 large heads cauliflower (about 3 lb. total)
- 1 Tbsp. olive oil
- ¼ tsp. salt
- ¼ tsp. black pepper
- ¼ tsp. ground cumin
- 1 recipe Jalapeño Creamed Spinach
- ¼ cup roasted, salted pepitas (pumpkin seeds)

CAULIFLOWER MAKES A GREAT STAND-IN FOR MEAT IN THIS VEGETARIAN DINNER. LOOK FOR THE FRESHEST CAULIFLOWER YOU CAN FIND: IT SHOULD HAVE TIGHT, COMPACT FLORETS WITH NO SIGNS OF YELLOWING OR BROWNING AND CRISP-LOOKING LEAVES AT THE BASE.

1. Preheat oven to 375°F. Remove outer leaves from the cauliflower. Carefully trim stem end, leaving core intact so florets are still attached. Turn cauliflower head core side down; using a chef's knife or large serrated knife, cut cauliflower vertically into four 1- to 1¼-inch-thick "steaks" (reserve ends and loose pieces for another use).

2. In an extra-large oven-going skillet heat oil over medium heat. Add cauliflower steaks; cook 4 to 6 minutes or until browned on both sides, turning once. Sprinkle with salt, pepper, and cumin. Transfer skillet to oven; roast, uncovered, 15 to 20 minutes or until tender. Remove cauliflower from skillet; cover to keep warm.

3. Prepare Jalapeño Creamed Spinach. Serve cauliflower steaks over creamed spinach. Sprinkle with pepitas. **MAKES 4 SERVINGS.**

JALAPEÑO CREAMED SPINACH Heat an extra-large skillet over medium heat. Add two 5- to 6-oz. pkg. fresh baby spinach, one package at a time, to hot skillet; stir until wilted. Transfer to a colander. Squeeze out excess liquid. In the same skillet heat 1 Tbsp. olive oil over medium heat. Add ½ cup chopped onion and 1 to 2 fresh jalapeño chile peppers, seeded and finely chopped (tip, page 51); cook 5 minutes or until tender. Add 1 cup heavy cream, and ¼ tsp. each salt and black pepper. Bring to boiling. Cook 3 to 5 minutes or until cream starts to thicken. Add the wilted spinach. Simmer until desired consistency.

PER SERVING *446 cal., 37 g fat (16 g sat. fat), 82 mg chol., 490 mg sodium, 23 g carb., 9 g fiber, 13 g pro.*

GARLICKY ZUCCHINI NOODLES

START TO FINISH 20 minutes

- 2 medium zucchini (about 10 oz. each), trimmed
- 3 Tbsp. walnut oil or olive oil
- 6 cloves garlic, smashed, peeled, and halved lengthwise
- ½ cup broken walnuts
- ½ tsp. kosher salt
- ¼ tsp. crushed red pepper
- 4 thin slices prosciutto or pancetta, torn
- 1 cup thinly sliced tart green apple
- 4 oz. soft goat cheese (chèvre), broken into pieces

FRESH TART APPLE SLICES GIVE THIS SPIRAL-CUT ZUCCHINI DISH A TANGY BITE. GRANNY SMITH OR BRAEBURN APPLES ARE GOOD OPTIONS.

1. Using a spiral vegetable slicer, cut zucchini into long thin strands (or using a vegetable peeler, cut lengthwise into thin ribbons). Cut through the strands with kitchen scissors to make them easier to serve.

2. In a very large skillet heat 2 Tbsp. of the oil over medium-high heat. Add garlic; cook and stir about 2 minutes or until softened and starting to brown. Add zucchini; cook and toss with tongs 1 minute. Transfer to a serving bowl. Add walnuts to skillet; cook and stir 1 to 2 minutes or until toasted. Add to bowl with zucchini. Sprinkle with salt and crushed red pepper.

3. Add remaining 1 Tbsp. oil to skillet. Add prosciutto; cook about 1 minute or until browned and crisp, turning once. Add to bowl with zucchini mixture. Add apple slices; toss gently to combine. Top with goat cheese.

MAKES 6 SERVINGS.

PER SERVING *217 cal., 18 g fat (4 g sat. fat), 13 mg chol., 405 mg sodium, 9 g carb., 2 g fiber, 8 g pro.*

SIDES

SKILLET-ROASTED VEGETABLES

PREP 20 minutes

COOK 22 minutes

- 8   oz. assorted baby beets
- 2   to 3 Tbsp. peanut oil
- 8   oz. tiny new potatoes and/or small fingerling potatoes, quartered
- 1   small sweet potato, peeled and cut into thin wedges
- 1   cup sugar snap pea pods or snow pea pods, trimmed if desired
- ¼   tsp. salt
- ⅛   tsp. freshly ground black pepper
- ¼   cup snipped fresh cilantro or Italian parsley
- 2   Tbsp. lemon juice
     Lemon wedges

THIS STOVE-TOP SAUTÉ OF BRIGHTLY COLORED VEGETABLES IS SIMPLY SEASONED WITH FRESHLY SQUEEZED LEMON JUICE AND CILANTRO. IF YOU CAN'T FIND BABY BEETS, YOU CAN CUT LARGER BEETS INTO QUARTERS.

1. Cut tops off beets and trim root ends; reserve ½ cup of the tops. Halve beets.

2. In an extra-large skillet heat oil over medium heat; add beets, quartered potatoes, and sweet potato. Cook, covered 10 minutes, turning occasionally. Uncover and cook 10 to 15 minutes or until vegetables are tender and browned on all sides, turning occasionally. Add pea pods; sprinkle with salt and pepper. Cover and cook 2 to 3 minutes more or until pea pods are crisp-tender.

3. Add the reserved beet greens, cilantro, and lemon juice to vegetables; toss gently to coat. Serve with lemon wedges. **MAKES 6 SERVINGS.**

PER SERVING *116 cal., 5 g fat (1 g sat. fat), 0 mg chol., 146 mg sodium, 17 g carb., 3 g fiber, 2 g pro.*

SKILLET-BROWNED BROCCOLI WITH PAN-TOASTED GARLIC

START TO FINISH 30 minutes

3 large broccoli heads with stem ends attached

3 Tbsp. olive oil

½ tsp. salt

¼ tsp. black pepper

Olive oil (optional)

3 Tbsp. thinly sliced garlic

Sea salt (optional)

WEIGHTING THE BROCCOLI WITH A SECOND SKILLET AS IT COOKS HELPS IT DEVELOP A CRISP, CARAMELIZED EDGE.

1. Cut broccoli heads lengthwise into 1-inch-thick slices, cutting from the bottom of the stems through the crown to preserve the shape of the broccoli (reserve any florets that fall away for another use). Brush both sides of broccoli slices with the 3 Tbsp. oil. Sprinkle with salt and pepper.

2. Heat an extra-large oven-going skillet over medium heat. Place half of the broccoli in the hot skillet and weight down with a medium heavy skillet. Cook 3 to 4 minutes or until browned. Turn slices over, weight them down, and cook 3 to 4 minutes more or until browned. (For more tender broccoli, cook over medium-low heat 5 to 6 minutes per side.) Remove broccoli from skillet; keep warm. Repeat with remaining broccoli.

3. If necessary, add additional oil to hot skillet; add garlic. Cook and stir over medium-low heat 2 minutes or until lightly toasted.

4. Sprinkle broccoli with the toasted garlic and, if desired, sea salt. **MAKES 8 SERVINGS.**

PER SERVING *79 cal., 5 g fat (1 g sat. fat), 0 mg chol., 174 mg sodium, 7 g carb., 2 g fiber, 3 g pro.*

SESAME GREEN BEANS WITH TERIYAKI GLAZE

START TO FINISH 30 minutes

1½ lb. green beans, trimmed

1 cup julienne carrots

¾ cup chicken broth

¼ cup soy sauce

¼ cup hoisin sauce

1 Tbsp. cornstarch

1 Tbsp. toasted sesame oil

3 Tbsp. canola oil

2 cups sliced stemmed fresh shiitake mushrooms

1 Tbsp. grated fresh ginger

4 cloves garlic, minced

2 Tbsp. snipped fresh basil

1 Tbsp. toasted sesame seeds (tip, page 15)

Fresh basil leaves

TOASTING THE SESAME SEEDS ENHANCES THEIR SAVORY, NUTTY FLAVOR. JUST PLACE THEM IN A DRY SKILLET OVER MEDIUM HEAT AND COOK, STIRRING AND SHAKING THE SKILLET OFTEN, UNTIL GOLDEN AND FRAGRANT.

1. Bring a large pot of salted water to boiling. Add green beans; return to boiling. Boil 4 minutes. Add carrots; boil 1 minute more. Drain well.

2. In a small bowl stir together chicken broth, soy sauce, hoisin sauce, cornstarch, and sesame oil.

3. In a large wok or an extra-large nonstick skillet heat canola oil over high heat. Add mushrooms, ginger, and garlic; cook and stir 3 minutes or until mushrooms are tender. Stir broth mixture and add to skillet; cook and stir 1 minute or until just thickened and bubbly. Stir in green beans and carrots and the 2 Tbsp. basil; heat through.

4. Sprinkle with toasted sesame seeds and top with additional fresh basil leaves. **MAKES 8 SERVINGS.**

PER SERVING *131 cal., 8 g fat (1 g sat. fat), 1 mg chol., 741 mg sodium, 14 g carb., 3 g fiber, 3 g pro.*

GREEN BEANS WITH SAGE AND MUSHROOMS

START TO FINISH **30 minutes**

2 lb. fresh green beans, trimmed if desired

2 Tbsp. olive oil

2 Tbsp. butter

3 to 4 cloves garlic, thinly sliced

12 oz. fresh mushrooms, such as cremini, button, porcini, or stemmed shiitake, halved lengthwise

3 Tbsp. snipped fresh sage

Coarse sea salt

Freshly ground black pepper

WHICHEVER VARIETY OF MUSHROOM YOU CHOOSE, LOOK FOR ONES THAT ARE FIRM, EVENLY COLORED, AND DRY LOOKING. AVOID THOSE THAT HAVE SOFT OR DARK BROWN POTS OR ONES THAT APPEAR WET.

1. In a large covered saucepan cook green beans in a small amount of boiling salted water 3 to 4 minutes or just until crisp-tender; drain. Immediately plunge beans into ice water; let stand 3 minutes. Drain.

2. In an extra-large skillet heat oil and butter over medium heat. Add garlic; cook and stir just until golden brown. Add mushrooms; cook 6 to 8 minutes or until tender, stirring occasionally. Add green beans. Cook 5 to 8 minutes or until heated through, stirring occasionally. Remove from heat. Stir in sage; season to taste with salt and pepper. **MAKES 8 SERVINGS.**

PER SERVING *112 cal., 6 g fat (2 g sat. fat), 8 mg chol., 150 mg sodium, 14 g carb., 4 g fiber, 3 g pro.*

SKILLET WHITE BEANS

PREP 20 minutes

COOK 25 minutes

3 Tbsp. butter

1 large sweet onion, such as Vidalia, Maui, or Walla Walla, halved and thinly sliced

½ cup maple syrup

⅓ cup white balsamic vinegar or lemon juice

2 Tbsp. packed brown sugar

2 Tbsp. snipped fresh sage

2 Tbsp. tomato paste

1 tsp. salt

½ tsp. freshly ground black pepper

2 15.5- to 16-oz. cans navy beans, rinsed and drained

2 15.5- to 16-oz. cans butter beans, rinsed and drained

1 15.5- to 16-oz. can garbanzo beans (chickpeas), rinsed and drained

Sour cream (optional)

Yellow, red, and/or green tomatoes, chopped (optional)

Fresh sage leaves (optional)

THESE DRESSED-UP BEANS HAVE AN IRRESISTIBLE TANGY-SWEET FLAVOR FROM MAPLE SYRUP, BROWN SUGAR, AND BALSAMIC VINEGAR. FRESH SAGE GIVES THEM A HINT OF EARTHINESS.

1. In an extra-large skillet heat butter over medium heat until melted. Add onion; cook 15 minutes or until very tender and golden, stirring occasionally. Stir in the next seven ingredients (through pepper). Add all of the beans; stir to combine.

2. Cook, covered, over medium heat 10 to 15 minutes or until heated through, stirring occasionally. Transfer to a serving bowl. If desired, top with sour cream, tomatoes, and sage leaves. **MAKES 12 SERVINGS.**

PER SERVING *246 cal., 7 g fat (4 g sat. fat), 21 mg chol., 570 mg sodium, 43 g carb., 9 g fiber, 10 g pro.*

BRINED SKILLET-ROASTED BRUSSELS SPROUTS

PREP 20 minutes

STAND 1 hour

ROAST 25 minutes at 350°F

1½ lb. fresh Brussels sprouts

8 cups cold water

½ cup kosher salt

¼ cup olive oil

1 tsp. mustard seeds

¼ tsp. cracked black pepper

¼ tsp. kosher salt (optional)

BRUSSELS SPROUTS ARE IN SEASON AND AT THEIR TASTIEST FROM EARLY FALL UNTIL SPRING. LOOK FOR ONES THAT HAVE SMALL TO MEDIUM COMPACT HEADS WITH NO BROWNING OR YELLOWING ON THE OUTER LEAVES.

1. Trim stems and remove any wilted outer leaves from Brussels sprouts. Halve any large sprouts.

2. For brine, in an extra-large bowl or deep container combine the cold water and the ½ cup salt, stirring until salt is completely dissolved. Add Brussels sprouts; make sure the sprouts are completely submerged (weight down with a plate if necessary). Let stand at room temperature 1 hour.

3. Preheat oven to 350°F. Drain Brussels sprouts; do not rinse. Transfer sprouts to an extra-large oven-going skillet or shallow roasting pan. Drizzle with oil; toss to coat. Roast 25 to 30 minutes or until tender, stirring once.

4. Meanwhile, in a small skillet heat mustard seeds over medium-low heat 5 minutes or until lightly toasted, shaking skillet occasionally. Remove seeds from skillet; crush slightly. Sprinkle crushed seeds, pepper, and, if desired, the ¼ tsp. salt over Brussels sprouts; toss gently to combine. **MAKES 6 SERVINGS.**

PER SERVING *126 cal., 9 g fat (1 g sat. fat), 0 mg chol., 346 mg sodium, 9 g carb., 4 g fiber, 4 g pro.*

CAULIFLOWER "COUSCOUS"

PREP **20 minutes**
STAND **10 minutes**
COOK **15 minutes**

- ¼ cup dried cranberries
- ¼ cup snipped dried apricots
- 2 medium heads cauliflower (1½ to 2 lb. each), cored and cut into florets (8 cups)
- 2 Tbsp. butter
- 1 Tbsp. olive oil
- 1 medium onion, halved and thinly sliced
- 2 cloves garlic, minced
- 1 5-oz. pkg. fresh baby spinach, chopped
- ½ cup toasted walnuts, chopped (tip, page 15)
- ½ tsp. salt
- ½ cup sliced green onions

PULSING THE CAULIFLOWER IN A FOOD PROCESSOR UNTIL FINELY CHOPPED GIVES IT THE APPEARANCE OF COUSCOUS. IT'S PERFECT FOR SERVING THOSE WHO ARE ON A GLUTEN-FREE DIET.

1. Place the dried cranberries and apricots in a small bowl. Cover with boiling water and let stand 10 minutes or until plump; drain well.
2. Meanwhile, place the cauliflower, in batches, in a food processor. Cover and pulse until crumbly and cauliflower resembles the texture of couscous.
3. In a very large skillet heat 1 Tbsp. of the butter and the olive oil over medium-high heat. Add the onion; cook and stir 3 minutes or until tender and just starting to brown. Add garlic; cook and stir 30 seconds more. Add cauliflower, spreading in an even layer. Cook 8 minutes or until cauliflower is golden, stirring occasionally.

4. Add drained cranberries and apricots, spinach, walnuts, and salt. Cook and stir until combined. Stir in the remaining 1 Tbsp. butter and the green onions. Toss until butter melts.
MAKES 8 SERVINGS.
To Make Ahead Prepare as directed through Step 3. Place in an airtight container; cover and chill up to 24 hours. To serve, reheat the cauliflower mixture in a very large lightly oiled skillet. Continue as directed. Or prepare the recipe as directed through Step 4. Cover and let stand at room temperature up to 4 hours. Serve at room temperature.
PER SERVING *139 cal., 8 g fat (3 g sat. fat), 8 mg chol., 217 mg sodium, 14 g carb., 4 g fiber, 4 g pro.*

SKILLET CORN

START TO FINISH **35 minutes**

- 4 slices bacon
- 2 cups fresh or frozen whole kernel corn
- 1 cup frozen shelled edamame
- 1 cup grape tomatoes or cherry tomatoes, halved
- ½ of a medium red onion, thinly sliced
- 2 Tbsp. snipped fresh cilantro
- 1 small fresh jalapeño chile pepper, seeded and finely chopped (tip, page 51)
- 1 Tbsp. olive oil
- ½ tsp. finely shredded lime peel
- 1 Tbsp. lime juice
- 2 cloves garlic, minced
- ¼ tsp. ground cumin
- ⅛ tsp. salt
- ⅛ tsp. chili powder

THIS UPDATED VERSION OF SUCCOTASH CALLS FOR EDAMAME–RATHER THAN TRADITIONAL LIMA BEANS–PLUS FRESH TOMATOES AND A JALAPEÑO CHILE PEPPER. IT'S TOPPED WITH TANGY LIME-GARLIC DRESSING AND CRISPY BACON.

1. In a large skillet cook bacon over medium heat until crisp. Remove bacon and drain on paper towels, reserving 2 Tbsp. drippings in skillet. Crumble bacon. Add corn and edamame to the reserved drippings. Cook and stir 3 to 4 minutes or just until vegetables are crisp-tender.

2. In a bowl combine corn mixture, tomatoes, red onion, cilantro, and jalapeño pepper.

3. For dressing, in a screw-top jar combine the remaining ingredients. Cover and shake well. Pour dressing over corn mixture; toss gently to coat. Sprinkle with crumbled bacon. **MAKES 6 SERVINGS.**

To Make Ahead Prepare as directed. Cover and chill up to 4 hours before serving. Serve at room temperature.

PER SERVING *182 cal., 11 g fat (3 g sat. fat), 9 mg chol., 160 mg sodium, 17 g carb., 3 g fiber, 7 g pro.*

SKILLET SCALLOPED CORN

START TO FINISH 25 minutes

- 3 Tbsp. butter
- ½ cup crushed rich round crackers
- 2 11-oz. cans whole kernel corn with sweet peppers, drained
- 2 7- to 8.75-oz. cans whole kernel corn with sweet peppers, whole kernel corn, or white whole kernel corn (shoepeg), drained
- 4 ¾-oz. slices process Swiss cheese, torn
- ⅔ cup milk
- ¼ tsp. onion powder
- ⅛ tsp. black pepper
- ⅔ cup crushed rich round crackers

Snipped fresh basil leaves and/or thinly sliced green onion (optional)

TO CRUSH THE CRACKERS FOR THE TOPPING, PLACE THEM IN A RESEALABLE PLASTIC BAG AND LIGHTLY POUND THEM WITH A MEAT MALLET OR ROLLING PIN.

1. For crumb topping, in a large skillet melt butter over medium heat. Add the ½ cup crushed crackers to the skillet. Cook and stir 3 minutes or until light brown. Remove from skillet.

2. In same skillet combine corn, cheese, milk, onion powder, and black pepper. Cook, stirring frequently, 10 minutes or until cheese melts and mixture is heated through. Stir in the ⅔ cup crushed crackers. Cook and stir 5 minutes more or until corn mixture is thickened. Transfer to a serving dish; sprinkle with crumb topping. If desired, sprinkle with basil and/or green onion.

MAKES 8 SERVINGS.

To Make Ahead Crush the ½ cup crackers as directed. Seal in a resealable heavy plastic bag. In a bowl combine corn, cheese, milk, onion powder, and black pepper. Cover; chill up to 48 hours. Prepare as directed.

PER SERVING 215 cal., 12 g fat (6 g sat. fat), 22 mg chol., 666 mg sodium, 24 g carb., 2 g fiber, 6 g pro.

SWEET-AND-SOUR CABBAGE

START TO FINISH **15 minutes**

- 3 Tbsp. packed brown sugar
- 3 Tbsp. vinegar
- 3 Tbsp. water
- 4 tsp. vegetable oil
- ¼ tsp. caraway seeds
- ¼ tsp. salt
- ⅛ tsp. black pepper
- 3 cups shredded red or green cabbage
- ¾ cup chopped apple

TO SHRED THE CABBAGE, CUT IT INTO WEDGES. REMOVE AND DISCARD THE CORE FROM EACH WEDGE. THINLY SLICE THE CORED CABBAGE INTO SHREDS, CUTTING CROSSWISE ACROSS THE GRAIN OF THE LEAVES.

1. In a large skillet combine the first seven ingredients (through black pepper). Cook 2 to 3 minutes or until hot and brown sugar is dissolved, stirring occasionally.

2. Stir in the cabbage and apple. Cook, covered, over medium-low heat 5 minutes or until cabbage is crisp-tender, stirring occasionally. **MAKES 4 SERVINGS.**

PER SERVING *109 cal., 5 g fat (1 g sat. fat), 0 mg chol., 163 mg sodium, 17 g carb., 2 g fiber, 1 g pro.*

SAUCY SKILLET MUSHROOMS

START TO FINISH 20 minutes

- 4 slices bacon, chopped
- 1 Tbsp. olive oil
- 1 lb. large fresh button mushrooms (1½ to 2 inches in diameter)
- 2 Tbsp. stone-ground mustard
- 2 Tbsp. snipped fresh Italian parsley

LOOK FOR EQUAL-SIZE BUTTON MUSHROOMS TO ENSURE THEY COOK AT THE SAME RATE. TO CLEAN THEM, GENTLY WIPE WITH A DAMP PAPER TOWEL. AVOID WASHING THEM IN WATER, WHICH WILL PREVENT THEM FROM BROWNING IN THE SKILLET.

1. In a large heavy skillet cook bacon over medium heat until crisp. Using a slotted spoon, remove bacon and drain on paper towels, reserving drippings in skillet.

2. Add oil to the reserved drippings. Add mushrooms; cook and stir over medium heat 1 to 2 minutes or just until mushrooms begin to brown. Cook, covered, 8 minutes or until tender, stirring occasionally. Stir in mustard; heat through. Sprinkle with crumbled bacon and parsley. **MAKES 4 SERVINGS.**

PER SERVING *214 cal., 19 g fat (6 g sat. fat), 25 mg chol., 356 mg sodium, 4 g carb., 1 g fiber, 8 g pro.*

MUSHROOM FRICASSEE WITH FRESH HERBS

PREP 25 minutes

COOK 17 minutes

STAND 5 minutes

2 lb. assorted fresh mushrooms, such as cremini, button, shiitake, chanterelle, porcini, oyster, and/or morels, cleaned and tough stems trimmed

2 Tbsp. walnut oil or extra-virgin olive oil

1 Tbsp. butter

½ cup finely chopped shallots

2 cloves garlic, minced

½ tsp. coarse sea salt

¼ tsp. black pepper

½ cup Madeira or chicken broth

½ cup heavy cream

1 Tbsp. snipped fresh chives

1 to 2 tsp. snipped fresh rosemary or ¼ to ½ tsp. dried rosemary, crushed

¼ cup snipped fresh Italian parsley

THESE FRENCH-STYLE STEWED MUSHROOMS CAN BE PREPARED WITH JUST ABOUT ANY VARIETY OF MUSHROOMS. A SPLASH OF MADEIRA—A PORTUGUESE FORTIFIED WINE—ENHANCES THEIR DEEP, RICH FLAVOR.

1. Leave small mushrooms whole, halve medium-size mushrooms, and quarter large mushrooms. (You will have about 12 cups mushrooms.) In an extra-large skillet heat 1 Tbsp. of the walnut oil and 1½ tsp. of the butter over medium heat. Add 6 cups of the mushrooms; cook 5 minutes or until the mushrooms begin to color, stirring occasionally. Using a slotted spoon, transfer cooked mushrooms to a large bowl. Repeat with the remaining mushrooms, oil, and butter. Add shallots, garlic, and reserved cooked mushrooms to the skillet; cook and stir 2 to 3 minutes more or until mushrooms are golden and shallots are tender. Stir in salt and pepper.

2. Remove from heat; add Madeira. Return to heat; simmer about 3 minutes or until the liquid is nearly gone. Stir in the cream, chives, and rosemary. Cook 2 minutes or until cream is slightly thickened. Remove from heat and let stand 5 minutes. Transfer to a serving bowl and sprinkle with parsley. **MAKES 6 SERVINGS.**

PER SERVING *193 cal., 14 g fat (6 g sat. fat), 32 mg chol., 231 mg sodium, 9 g carb., 2 g fiber, 6 g pro.*

SPICY HERB-FRIED GREEN TOMATOES

PREP 35 minutes

COOK 4 minutes

1   8-oz. carton sour cream

6   cloves garlic, minced

1   Tbsp. snipped fresh cilantro

⅛   tsp. salt

¼   cup milk

2   cups crushed potato chips (about 5 oz.)

1   Tbsp. snipped fresh thyme

½   tsp. black pepper

¼   tsp. cayenne pepper

½   cup all-purpose flour

2   large firm green tomatoes (about 1 lb. total), sliced ¼ inch thick

3   Tbsp. butter

3   Tbsp. olive oil

CRUSHED POTATO CHIPS PROVIDE A CRISP COATING FOR FRIED GREEN TOMATOES. FOR ANOTHER OPTION, TRY CRUSHED CRACKERS OR PANKO BREAD CRUMBS.

1. In a bowl combine sour cream, garlic, cilantro, and salt. Reserve half of the mixture for serving. Place the remaining mixture in a shallow dish and whisk in milk until combined. In another shallow dish combine crushed potato chips, thyme, black pepper, and cayenne pepper. Place flour in a third shallow dish.

2. Dip tomato slices in flour, turning to coat; shake off excess. Dip in sour cream-milk mixture, then in potato chip mixture.

3. In an extra-large skillet heat 2 Tbsp. of the butter and 2 Tbsp. of the oil over medium heat. Add half of the coated tomato slices; cook 4 minutes or until crisp and golden, turning once. Drain on paper towels. Repeat with remaining butter, olive oil, and tomato slices. Serve with reserved sour cream mixture.

MAKES 6 SERVINGS.

PER SERVING *376 cal., 29 g fat (12 g sat. fat), 36 mg chol., 258 mg sodium, 26 g carb., 2 g fiber, 5 g pro.*

ZUCCHINI FRITTERS WITH CAPER MAYONNAISE

PREP 35 minutes

COOK 8 minutes

8   oz. zucchini, coarsely
    shredded

½   tsp. salt

1   lemon

⅓   cup mayonnaise

1   Tbsp. capers, drained and
    coarsely chopped

1   tsp. snipped fresh lemon
    thyme or thyme

⅛   tsp. black pepper

8   oz. russet potatoes

½   cup all-purpose flour

½   tsp. baking powder

⅛   tsp. cayenne pepper

1   egg, lightly beaten

2   Tbsp. olive oil

ZUCCHINI CONTAINS A SUBSTANTIAL AMOUNT OF WATER. SPRINKLING THE SHREDDED ZUCCHINI WITH SALT BEFORE COMBINING IT WITH THE OTHER INGREDIENTS ENCOURAGES IT TO RELEASE EXCESS MOISTURE, PREVENTING THE BATTER FROM GETTING TOO WATERY.

1. Line a 15×10-inch baking pan with several layers of paper towels. Spread zucchini on paper towels; sprinkle with salt. Top with another layer of paper towels. Let stand 15 minutes, pressing occasionally to release moisture. Meanwhile, remove 1 tsp. zest and squeeze 2 tsp. juice from lemon.

2. For caper mayonnaise, in a bowl stir together mayonnaise, the lemon juice, capers, lemon thyme, and black pepper.

3. Transfer zucchini to a large bowl. Peel and finely shred the potatoes;* add to the zucchini. Add the lemon peel, flour, baking powder, and cayenne pepper; toss to combine. Stir in egg until combined.

4. In a large nonstick skillet heat 2 tsp. of the olive oil over medium-high heat. Working in batches, drop batter by slightly rounded tablespoons into the hot skillet. Use a spatula to flatten into patties. Cook 4 to 5 minutes per side or until golden brown (reduce heat to medium if browning too quickly). Keep fritters warm in a 200°F oven while cooking remaining fritters, adding more oil as needed. Serve fritters with caper mayonnaise. **MAKES 5 SERVINGS.**

*Tip Don't shred the potatoes ahead of time or they will darken.

PER SERVING *243 cal., 18 g fat (3 g sat. fat), 43 mg chol., 443 mg sodium, 18 g carb., 1 g fiber, 4 g pro.*

SKILLET SALT-ROASTED POTATOES

PREP 15 minutes

COOK 35 minutes

STAND 10 minutes

2 lb. red and/or yellow small new potatoes

2 cups kosher salt

1 to 2 Tbsp. fennel seeds or caraway seeds (optional)

1 Tbsp. olive oil

A THICK LAYER OF INEXPENSIVE COARSE KOSHER SALT IS USED TO BOTH SEASON THE POTATOES AND TO CREATE AND HOLD AN EVEN HEAT AS THEY ROAST ON THE STOVE-TOP.

1. Scrub potatoes. Pour salt into the bottom of an extra-large heavy oven-going skillet or Dutch oven, spreading evenly. Heat over medium heat 5 minutes or until hot. If desired, sprinkle with fennel seeds.

2. Add potatoes to hot salt in skillet, slightly pressing potatoes into salt. Cover skillet. Cook over medium heat 35 to 40 minutes or until potatoes are tender. Remove skillet from heat. Let stand, covered, 5 minutes.

3. Remove potatoes from skillet with tongs and brush excess salt from potatoes (reserve salt mixture). Transfer potatoes to a serving platter; drizzle with oil. Cover with foil and let stand 5 minutes. Serve with reserved salt mixture.

MAKES 4 SERVINGS.

PER SERVING *129 cal., 3 g fat (0 g sat. fat), 0 mg chol., 331 mg sodium, 25 g carb., 3 g fiber, 3 g pro.*

APPLE-THYME SAUTÉ

START TO FINISH 15 minutes

- 1 Tbsp. butter
- 2 medium Granny Smith and/or Rome Beauty apples, cored and cut into ½-inch wedges (about 2½ cups)
- ⅓ cup sliced shallots
- 1 Tbsp. snipped fresh thyme or 1 tsp. dried thyme, crushed
- 1 Tbsp. lemon juice
- ¼ tsp. salt
- ⅛ tsp. black pepper

FRESH THYME AND SHALLOTS COMBINE WITH JUST-TENDER APPLES FOR A SWEET-SAVORY SIDE DISH. ALTERNATELY, TRY FRESH ROSEMARY OR SAGE IN PLACE OF THE THYME.

1. In a large skillet melt butter over medium heat. Add apples, shallots, and thyme. Cook, covered, 5 minutes or just until apples are tender, stirring occasionally. Stir in lemon juice, salt, and pepper. **MAKES 4 SERVINGS.**

PER SERVING *84 cal., 3 g fat (2 g sat. fat), 8 mg chol., 168 mg sodium, 15 g carb., 2 g fiber, 1 g pro.*

SKILLET CORN BREAD 4 WAYS

PREP 15 minutes

BAKE 18 minutes at 425°F

- 1 Tbsp. butter
- 1 Tbsp. vegetable oil
- 1 cup all-purpose flour
- 1 cup cornmeal
- 2 Tbsp. sugar
- 1 Tbsp. baking powder
- ½ tsp. salt
- 2 eggs, lightly beaten
- 1 cup milk
- ¼ cup vegetable oil or shortening, melted
- ½ cup butter, softened (optional)
- 2 Tbsp. honey (optional)

MAKE TRADITIONAL CORN BREAD USING THE BASE RECIPE, OR MIX THINGS UP A BIT BY TRYING ONE OF FOUR CREATIVE VARIATIONS.

1. Preheat oven to 425°F. Place the 1 Tbsp. butter and the 1 Tbsp. oil in a large heavy oven-going skillet. Heat in oven 5 minutes; do not heat longer or mixture may burn.

2. Meanwhile, in a bowl stir together flour, cornmeal, sugar, baking powder, and salt. Make a well in the center of flour mixture. In a bowl combine eggs, milk, and the ¼ cup oil. Add egg mixture all at once in well of flour mixture. Stir just until moistened.

3. Pour batter into the prepared skillet, spreading evenly. Return skillet to oven. Bake 18 to 20 minutes or until a wooden toothpick inserted near the center comes out clean.

4. Meanwhile, if desired, prepare honey butter. In a bowl beat the ½ cup softened butter with a mixer on medium 30 seconds. Add honey; beat on high 1 minute or until fluffy.

5. If desired, serve hot corn bread with honey butter. **MAKES 8 WEDGES.**

PER WEDGE *255 cal., 12 g fat (3 g sat. fat), 53 mg chol., 375 mg sodium, 31 g carb., 1 g fiber, 5 g pro.*

BACON-GREEN ONION CORN BREAD Prepare as directed, except stir ½ cup crumbled, crisp-cooked bacon and ⅓ cup sliced green onions into batter. If desired, sprinkle with additional sliced green onions before serving.

PER WEDGE *299 cal., 16 g fat (4 g sat. fat), 62 mg chol., 573 mg sodium, 31 g carb., 1 g fiber, 8 g pro.*

CHEESY CHIPOTLE CORN BREAD Prepare as directed, except stir ½ cup shredded sharp cheddar cheese (2 oz.) and 1 canned chipotle pepper in adobo sauce, finely chopped, into batter.

PER WEDGE *285 cal., 15 g fat (4 g sat. fat), 60 mg chol., 31 g carb., 1 g fiber, 7 g pro.*

CRANBERRY-TANGERINE CORN BREAD Prepare as directed, except stir ½ cup dried cranberries and 1 tsp. tangerine or orange zest into batter.

PER WEDGE *278 cal., 12 g fat (3 g sat. fat), 53 mg chol., 375 mg sodium, 37 g carb., 2 g fiber, 5 g pro.*

SWEET CORN AND HERB CORN BREAD Prepare as directed, except stir ½ cup fresh corn kernels or frozen whole kernel corn, thawed; 2 Tbsp. snipped fresh Italian parsley; 1 Tbsp. snipped fresh chives; and 2 tsp. snipped fresh thyme into batter.

PER WEDGE *264 cal., 12 g fat (3 g sat. fat), 53 mg chol., 377 mg sodium, 33 g carb., 1 g fiber, 6 g pro.*

DOUBLE-OLIVE NO-KNEAD SKILLET FOCACCIA

PREP 15 minutes
RISE 3 hours 30 minutes
BAKE 30 minutes at 400°F
COOL 15 minutes

3¾ cups all-purpose flour

1¾ tsp. kosher salt, divided

½ tsp. active dry yeast

1½ cups warm water

¼ cup chopped Kalamata olives

2 Tbsp. chopped green olives

2 tsp. fresh rosemary or thyme leaves

2 cloves garlic, sliced

2 Tbsp. olive oil, divided

THE DOUGH FOR THIS BREAD IS VERY SOFT AND SLIGHTLY STICKY, SO BE SURE TO USE WELL-FLOURED HANDS WHEN TRANSFERRING IT FROM THE BOWL TO THE SKILLET.

1. In a large bowl combine 2¾ cups of the flour, 1½ tsp. of the salt, and the yeast. Add the warm water. Stir until flour mixture is moistened. (The dough will be sticky and soft.) Cover bowl with waxed paper; let rest at room temperature 2 hours.

2. Lightly grease an extra-large oven-going skillet. Using a fork, stir the remaining 1 cup flour into the dough. Gather dough with your hands. Spread dough slightly in the skillet. Place a lightly greased piece of plastic wrap over the dough, greased side down. Let rise at room temperature 1½ to 2 hours or until puffy.

3. Preheat oven to 400°F. Uncover dough. Sprinkle with olives, rosemary, and garlic; drizzle with 1 Tbsp. of the olive oil and sprinkle with remaining ¼ tsp. salt. Cook over medium-high heat 3 minutes. Transfer to oven and bake 30 minutes or until golden brown. Let cool in pan on a wire rack 15 minutes. Drizzle with remaining 1 Tbsp. olive oil and serve warm.

MAKES 10 WEDGES.

PER WEDGE *204 cal., 4 g fat (0 g sat. fat), 0 mg chol., 413 mg sodium, 36 g carb., 2 g fiber, 5 g pro.*

CHEDDAR-BACON BUTTERMILK BISCUITS

PREP 15 minutes

BAKE 18 minutes at 425°F

COOKING THE BISCUITS IN A PREHEATED SKILLET RESULTS IN A CRISPY, DEEP BROWN CRUST.

3	cups all-purpose flour
1	Tbsp. baking powder
1	Tbsp. sugar
1	tsp. salt
¾	tsp. cream of tartar
¾	cup cold butter, cut up
¾	cup shredded cheddar cheese (3 oz.)
8	slices bacon, crisp-cooked and crumbled
1¼	cups buttermilk
1	Tbsp. vegetable oil
	Milk

1. Preheat oven to 425°F. Place an extra-large oven-going skillet in the oven to preheat.

2. In a very large bowl combine flour, baking powder, sugar, salt, and cream of tartar. Using a pastry blender, cut butter into flour mixture until mixture resembles coarse crumbs. Stir in the cheese and bacon. Make a well in the center of the flour mixture. Add buttermilk all at once. Using a fork, stir just until mixture is moistened.

3. Turn dough out onto a lightly floured surface. Knead dough by folding and gently pressing it just until dough holds together. Pat or lightly roll dough until 1-inch thick. Cut dough with a floured 2½-inch biscuit cutter into 12 rounds; reroll scraps as necessary and dip cutter into flour between cuts.

4. Carefully remove hot skillet from oven and add oil; use a pastry brush to coat bottom and sides of skillet. Arrange dough rounds in the hot skillet. Brush with milk. Bake 18 to 22 minutes or until golden. Serve warm. **MAKES 12 BISCUITS.**

PER BISCUIT *296 cal., 17 g fat (10 g sat. fat), 45 mg chol., 569 mg sodium, 27 g carb., 1 g fiber, 8 g pro.*

DESSERTS

BLACKBERRY CLAFOUTI

PREP 25 minutes

BAKE 10 minutes at 375°F +
25 minutes at 350°F

- 1 Tbsp. butter, softened
- 3 eggs
- ½ cup granulated sugar
- ¾ cup whole milk
- ½ cup heavy cream
- ½ cup all-purpose flour
- 2 Tbsp. orange liqueur or
  orange juice
- 2 tsp. finely shredded
  orange peel
- 1½ tsp. vanilla
- ¼ tsp. salt
- 3 cups fresh or frozen
  blackberries*

  Powdered sugar

  Crème fraîche or soft
  whipped cream

CLAFOUTI IS A TRADITIONAL COUNTRY-STYLE FRENCH DESSERT COMPOSED OF A LAYER OF FRESH FRUIT—BLACKBERRIES, IN THIS CASE—TOPPED WITH BATTER. SOME STYLES ARE MORE CAKELIKE WHILE OTHERS ARE MORE LIKE A PUDDING.

1. Preheat oven to 375°F. Using the softened butter, butter a large heavy oven-going skillet, six mini skillets, or six 6- to 8-oz. ramekins. In a bowl beat eggs and granulated sugar with a mixer 3 minutes or until light and lemon color. Stir in the next seven ingredients (through salt).

2. Arrange berries in the prepared skillet. Carefully pour batter over berries. Bake 10 minutes. Reduce oven temperature to 350°F. Bake 25 to 30 minutes more for large skillet or 20 to 25 minutes more for smaller pans or until filling is set and top is golden brown.

3. Sprinkle with powdered sugar and serve warm with crème fraîche. **MAKES 6 SERVINGS.**

*Tip If using frozen berries, arrange frozen berries on a baking sheet lined with paper towels. Thaw 10 to 15 minutes (berries will not be fully thawed). Carefully transfer to skillet (try not to break berries).

PER SERVING *363 cal., 20 g fat (12 g sat. fat), 155 mg chol., 178 mg sodium, 37 g carb., 4 g fiber, 7 g pro.*

DOUBLE-BERRY SKILLET COBBLER

PREP 20 minutes
COOK 8 minutes
BAKE 15 minutes at 400°F
COOL 45 minutes

1⅓ cups sugar

3 Tbsp. cornstarch

½ tsp. salt

½ tsp. ground cinnamon

¼ cup water

5 cups fresh or frozen blackberries, thawed

¾ cup fresh or frozen blueberries, thawed

½ tsp. lemon juice

2 Tbsp. butter

1 12-oz. pkg. refrigerated flaky buttermilk refrigerated biscuits

1 Tbsp. sugar

½ tsp. ground cinnamon

1 Tbsp. milk

Vanilla ice cream (optional)

PURCHASED BUTTERMILK BISCUIT DOUGH MAKES EASY WORK OF THIS BLACKBERRY AND BLUEBERRY COBBLER. ALLOW THE COBBLER TO COOL FOR AT LEAST 45 MINUTES SO THAT IT CAN SET UP BEFORE SERVING.

1. Preheat oven to 400°F. In a nonreactive medium oven-going skillet stir together the first four ingredients (through cinnamon). Add the water. Cook and stir over medium heat until sugar is mostly dissolved. Add berries, lemon juice, and butter. Cook, stirring frequently, until butter melts and mixture is thickened and bubbly.

2. Remove skillet from heat. Split each biscuit in half horizontally and arrange the biscuit halves over the hot berry mixture, overlapping slightly. (Bake any leftover biscuits separately.)

3. In a bowl stir together the 1 Tbsp. sugar and ½ tsp. cinnamon. Brush biscuit tops with milk and sprinkle with cinnamon-sugar. Bake 15 minutes or until biscuits are golden brown. Cool on a wire rack 45 minutes before serving. Serve warm with vanilla ice cream, if desired.

MAKES 8 SERVINGS.

PER SERVING *353 cal., 9 g fat (3 g sat. fat), 8 mg chol., 569 mg sodium, 67 g carb., 6 g fiber, 4 g pro.*

CRANBERRY ORANGE UPSIDE-DOWN SPICE CAKE

PREP 20 minutes
BAKE 35 minutes at 350°F
COOL 3 minutes

1½   cups all-purpose flour
1   tsp. baking powder
½   tsp. ground ginger
½   tsp. ground cinnamon
¼   tsp. baking soda
¼   tsp. salt
3   Tbsp. butter
¾   cup packed brown sugar
1   11-oz. can mandarin orange sections, drained
1   cup fresh or frozen cranberries
2   eggs, lightly beaten
¾   cup plain Greek yogurt or sour cream
¾   cup granulated sugar
6   Tbsp. butter, melted
1   tsp. vanilla

FRESH CRANBERRIES ARE IN SEASON FROM OCTOBER TO DECEMBER, MAKING THIS CAKE PERFECT FOR THE HOLIDAYS. IT TASTES AMAZING ON ITS OWN, BUT YOU CAN SEND IT OVER THE TOP BY SERVING WITH VANILLA ICE CREAM, CRÈME FRAÎCHE, OR SWEETENED WHIPPED CREAM.

1. Preheat oven to 350°F. In a large bowl stir together the first six ingredients (through salt). Add the 3 Tbsp. butter to a large heavy oven-going skillet. Place skillet in oven 3 to 5 minutes or just until butter is melted. Carefully remove from oven and tip skillet to coat sides with butter.

2. Sprinkle brown sugar over bottom of skillet. Arrange orange sections over brown sugar. Top with cranberries.

3. In a bowl combine the remaining ingredients. Add flour mixture to egg mixture, one-third at a time, stirring just until combined after each addition. Spoon batter into skillet, spreading to cover fruit.

4. Bake 35 to 40 minutes or until a wooden toothpick inserted in center comes out clean. Cool in skillet on a wire rack 3 to 4 minutes. Run a knife around edges of cake to loosen. Invert onto a platter. Replace any fruit that remains in skillet. Serve warm or at room temperature. **MAKES 8 SERVINGS.**

PER SERVING *408 cal., 15 g fat (9 g sat. fat), 84 mg chol., 320 mg sodium, 63 g carb., 2 g fiber, 6 g pro.*

MIXED BERRY CRISP

PREP 25 minutes

BAKE 30 minutes at 350°F

COOL 30 minutes

3 cups mixed fresh berries, such as blueberries, blackberries, and/or raspberries

⅓ cup granulated sugar

4 tsp. quick-cooking tapioca

½ tsp. ground cinnamon

½ tsp. ground ginger

½ cup crushed amaretti cookies

¼ cup all-purpose flour

2 Tbsp. sliced almonds

2 Tbsp. packed brown sugar

¼ cup butter

1 Tbsp. butter, softened

Vanilla ice cream

Mixed fresh berries, such as blueberries, blackberries, and/or raspberries (optional)

CRUSHED AMARETTI COOKIES GIVE THIS CRISP A SWEET ALMOND FLAVOR. YOU COULD USE GINGERSNAPS OR VANILLA WAFERS, IF YOU PREFER.

1. Preheat oven to 350°F. In a bowl combine the first five ingredients (through ginger). Let stand 15 minutes, stirring occasionally.

2. For topping, in a bowl combine crushed amaretti, flour, almonds, and brown sugar. Using a pastry blender, cut in the ¼ cup butter until mixture resembles coarse crumbs.

3. Using the 1 Tbsp. softened butter, generously butter a medium heavy oven-going skillet or two individual 10- to 12-oz. heavy oven-going skillets or casseroles. Pour berry filling in skillet(s). Sprinkle with topping.

4. Bake until bubbly and topping is golden brown. Allow 30 minutes for large skillet or 20 minutes for small skillets.

5. Cool 30 minutes before serving. Serve warm with ice cream and, if desired, additional berries. **MAKES 4 SERVINGS.**

Grilling Directions You need to use a cast-iron skillet(s) or casserole for grilling. Prepare as directed through Step 3, except do not preheat oven. For a charcoal grill, arrange medium-hot coals around edges of grill, leaving center of grill with no coals. Test for medium heat above center of grill. Place skillet(s) in center of grill rack (not over the coals). Cover and grill until bubbly and topping is golden brown. Allow 35 minutes for large skillet or 20 minutes for small skillets. (For a gas grill, preheat grill. Reduce heat to medium. Adjust for indirect cooking. Place skillet(s) over burner that is off. Grill as directed.) Serve as directed in Step 5.

PER SLICE *544 cal., 25 g fat (14 g sat. fat), 70 mg chol., 169 mg sodium, 75 g carb., 5 g fiber, 6 g pro.*

PLUM-BERRY SKILLET COBBLER WITH CINNAMON ICE CREAM

PREP 25 minutes
BAKE 35 minutes at 375°F
COOL 30 minutes

WHEN PURCHASING PLUMS FOR THIS DESSERT, LOOK FOR FRUIT THAT IS EVEN IN COLOR, PLUMP, AND UNBLEMISHED. THEY SHOULD BE FIRM BUT YIELD JUST SLIGHTLY TO PALM PRESSURE.

1½ cups cranberries

½ cup dried tart red cherries

½ cup water

⅔ cup granulated sugar

3 Tbsp. all-purpose flour

2 lb. large plums, pitted and cut into bite-size chunks

1½ cups all-purpose flour

½ cup rolled oats

2 Tbsp. packed brown sugar

1½ tsp. baking powder

½ tsp. salt

½ tsp. cream of tartar

6 Tbsp. butter

½ cup milk

Cinnamon ice cream (optional)

1. For filling, in a large oven-going skillet combine cranberries, cherries, and the water. Stir in granulated sugar and the 3 Tbsp. flour. Cook and stir over medium heat until hot and bubbly. Stir in plums; cover to keep warm.
2. Preheat oven to 375°F. In a large bowl combine the next six ingredients (through cream of tartar). Using a pastry blender, cut in butter until mixture resembles coarse crumbs. Make a well in the center of flour mixture. Add milk all at once. Using a fork, stir just until moistened.

3. Lightly flatten dough then cut into about 12 squares; place on filling in skillet. Brush dough with additional milk; sprinkle with additional brown sugar.
4. Bake 35 to 40 minutes or until topping is golden brown and filling is bubbly. (If necessary, cover loosely with foil the last 10 minutes of baking to prevent overbrowning.) Cool 30 minutes before serving. If desired, serve with cinnamon ice cream. **MAKES 8 SERVINGS.**

PER SERVING *526 cal., 19 g fat (11 g sat. fat), 73 mg chol., 358 mg sodium, 85 g carb., 5 g fiber, 8 g pro.*

CARAMELIZED APPLE SKILLET TART

PREP 20 minutes

COOK 20 minutes

BAKE 30 minutes at 375°F

COOL 25 minutes

½ cup butter

6 cups thickly sliced cooking apples, peeled if desired

⅔ cup sugar

1½ cups all-purpose flour

3 Tbsp. sugar

½ cup butter

1 egg, lightly beaten

Cold water

Vanilla ice cream (optional)

DOES IT MATTER WHAT KIND OF APPLES GO INTO THIS TART? YES! CHOOSE TART-SWEET APPLES THAT WILL HOLD THEIR SHAPE WHEN COOKED. TOP CHOICES INCLUDE GRANNY SMITH, HONEYCRISP, JONATHAN, AND BRAEBURN.

1. Preheat oven to 375°F. In a large oven-going skillet melt ½ cup butter over medium heat. Stir in apples and the ⅔ cup sugar. Cook over medium heat until bubbly, stirring occasionally. Reduce heat to medium-low. Cook, uncovered, 20 minutes more or until apples are very tender, stirring occasionally. Remove from heat.

2. Meanwhile, in a bowl stir together flour and the 3 Tbsp. sugar. Using a pastry blender, cut in ½ cup butter until pea-size. Using a fork, stir in egg and 1 to 2 Tbsp. cold water until flour mixture begins to come together. Form into a ball.

3. On a lightly floured surface, use your hands to slightly flatten pastry. Roll pastry into a 10-inch circle. Cut slits in the pastry and transfer to cover apple filling in skillet. If necessary, carefully fold under edges of pastry.

4. Bake 30 minutes or until the pastry is golden brown and filling is bubbly. Cool on a wire rack 25 minutes before serving. Serve warm tart with ice cream, if desired. **MAKES 12 SERVINGS.**

PER SERVING *289 cal., 17 g fat (10 g sat. fat), 61 mg chol., 173 mg sodium, 33 g carb., 1 g fiber, 3 g pro.*

PEACH-BLUEBERRY CRISP

PREP **20 minutes**

BAKE **25 minutes at 350°F**

- 3 cups sliced, peeled fresh peaches
- 2 cups fresh blueberries
- ½ tsp. ground nutmeg
- ½ cup regular rolled oats
- ½ cup chopped almonds
- ⅓ cup packed brown sugar
- ¼ cup flaked coconut
- ½ tsp. ground cinnamon
- ¼ cup butter, melted
- 1 cup frozen light whipped dessert topping, thawed

  Grated whole nutmeg

MAKE THIS SUMMERY DESSERT WHEN PEACHES COME INTO SEASON IN LATE SPRING AND SUMMER. CHOOSE ONES THAT ARE INTENSELY FRAGRANT WITH NO BROWN SPOTS AND GIVE JUST SLIGHTLY TO PALM PRESSURE.

1. Preheat oven to 350°F. In three small oven-going skillets or a 2-qt. baking dish combine peaches and blueberries. Sprinkle with the ground nutmeg.

2. For topping, in a bowl stir together the next five ingredients (through cinnamon). Drizzle with melted butter; toss gently to combine. Sprinkle topping over fruit.

3. Bake 25 to 35 minutes or until peaches are tender and topping is golden. Cover loosely with foil the last 10 minutes of baking to prevent overbrowning.

4. Serve warm with whipped topping and sprinkle with grated nutmeg. **MAKES 6 SERVINGS.**

PER SERVING *322 cal., 16 g fat (8 g sat. fat), 20 mg chol., 82 mg sodium, 43 g carb., 5 g fiber, 5 g pro.*

BANANA-FIG SKILLET CRISP

PREP **15 minutes**

COOK **14 minutes**

¼ cup regular rolled oats

¼ cup chopped raw macadamia nuts

2 Tbsp. shredded or flaked coconut

2 Tbsp. granulated sugar

1½ Tbsp. butter

⅛ tsp. ground ginger

3 medium to large bananas, cut crosswise into ½-inch slices

½ cup dried calimyrna or Kalamata figs, stemmed and chopped (about 3 oz.)

¼ cup butter

¼ cup packed brown sugar

1 tsp. grated fresh ginger or ¼ tsp. ground ginger

¼ tsp. ground cinnamon

2 Tbsp. rum or water

2 Tbsp. honey

1½ cups vanilla or coconut ice cream

READY IN LESS THAN A HALF-HOUR, THIS NO-BAKE FRUIT CRISP MAKES A PERFECT LAST-MINUTE DESSERT. GIVE IT AN EXTRA BOOST OF TROPICAL FLAVOR BY TOPPING EACH SERVING WITH COCONUT ICE CREAM.

1. In a medium heavy oven-going skillet cook oats and macadamia nuts over medium to medium-high heat 2 to 3 minutes or until nuts are very lightly browned, stirring frequently. Add coconut. Cook and stir 2 to 3 minutes more or until mixture is toasted. Add granulated sugar, the 1½ Tbsp. butter, and ⅛ tsp. ginger; stir until butter is melted and mixture is evenly coated. Remove from heat. Transfer to a bowl.

2. In the same skillet cook the next six ingredients (through cinnamon) over medium heat 3 to 5 minutes or until bananas and figs are just softened, gently stirring occasionally. Remove from heat. Add rum and honey. Return to medium heat; cook 1 minute more, gently stirring to coat the fruit well. Remove from heat.

3. Sprinkle oat topping over fruit filling in skillet. Serve warm topped with ice cream.

MAKES 4 SERVINGS.

PER SERVING *694 cal., 37 g fat (20 g sat. fat), 116 mg chol., 201 mg sodium, 87 g carb., 6 g fiber, 6 g pro.*

GRILLED DULCE DE LECHE PEACH PIE

PREP 30 minutes

GRILL 45 minutes

COOL 2 hours

3½ lb. peaches, halved and pitted

1 Tbsp. canola oil

½ cup granulated sugar

3 Tbsp. cornstarch

1 Tbsp. lemon juice

1 14.1-oz. pkg. rolled refrigerated unbaked piecrust (2 crusts)

¼ cup dulce de leche

½ tsp. kosher salt

1 egg, lightly beaten

Coarse sugar

Ice cream (optional)

Fresh mint leaves (optional)

AMAZE GUESTS AT YOUR NEXT BARBECUE BY PREPARING THIS SEASONAL PIE ON THE GRILL. THANKS TO PURCHASED PIECRUST, IT'S A SNAP TO PREPARE.

1. Brush peach halves with oil. Prepare grill for indirect heat. Place peach halves, cut sides down, on grill rack over medium heat. Grill, covered, 3 minutes. Cut peach halves into ½-inch-thick slices. In an extra-large bowl toss peaches with granulated sugar, cornstarch, and lemon juice.

2. Grease a medium cast-iron* skillet and line with one of the piecrusts. Spoon peaches into skillet; spoon dulce de leche in mounds over filling. Sprinkle with salt. Cut slits in second crust and place over filling. Tuck dough down sides of skillet. Crimp edge as desired. Brush pastry with egg and sprinkle with coarse sugar.

3. Place skillet on grill rack over indirect medium heat. Grill, covered, 45 to 50 minutes or until crust is golden and filling is bubbly, rotating skillet once. Cool on a wire rack at least 2 hours before serving. If desired, serve with ice cream and top with mint leaves. **MAKES 8 SLICES.**

*Tip You must use a cast-iron skillet for this recipe because it is cooked on the grill.

PER SLICE *410 cal., 17 g fat (6 g sat. fat), 31 mg chol., 352 mg sodium, 65 g carb., 3 g fiber, 4 g pro.*

LEMON-OLIVE OIL CAKE

PREP 20 minutes

BAKE 25 minutes at 375°F

COOL 15 minutes

1 Tbsp. butter, softened

½ cup granulated sugar

½ cup slivered almonds, toasted (tip, page 15)

2 cups all-purpose flour

4 tsp. finely shredded lemon peel

1 Tbsp. baking powder

½ tsp. salt

3 eggs, lightly beaten

1 cup buttermilk

6 Tbsp. lemon juice

¼ cup olive oil

½ tsp. almond extract

2 cups seasonal fresh fruit such as sliced or cut-up peaches, nectarines, or plums; Cara Cara or blood orange sections; fresh berries; and/or pitted sweet cherries

2 Tbsp. granulated sugar

Powdered sugar (optional)

ALTHOUGH OLIVE OIL IS USUALLY RESERVED FOR SAVORY APPLICATIONS, ITS EARTHY FLAVOR MESHES BEAUTIFULLY WITH TANGY LEMON AND ALMONDS IN THIS NOT-TOO-SWEET CAKE. TOP IT WITH FRESH FRUIT JUST BEFORE SERVING.

1. Preheat oven to 375°F. Using the butter, generously butter a medium heavy oven-going skillet or a 9-inch round cake pan.

2. In a food processor combine the ½ cup granulated sugar and the almonds. Cover and process until fine. Transfer to a large bowl. Stir in flour, lemon peel, baking powder, and salt until combined. Make a well in the center of flour mixture.

3. In a bowl whisk together eggs, buttermilk, 3 Tbsp. of the lemon juice, the oil, and almond extract. Add to flour mixture all at once, stirring just until combined. Pour batter into prepared skillet; spread evenly.

4. Bake 25 minutes for a skillet or 30 minutes for a cake pan or until a wooden toothpick inserted in the center comes out clean. Cool cake in skillet on a wire rack at least 15 minutes before serving.

5. Meanwhile, in a bowl combine fruit, remaining 3 Tbsp. lemon juice, and the 2 Tbsp. granulated sugar. If desired, lightly sprinkle cake with powdered sugar. Serve warm or at room temperature with fruit. **MAKES 8 SERVINGS.**

PER SERVING *350 cal., 14 g fat (3 g sat. fat), 75 mg chol., 401 mg sodium, 49 g carb., 3 g fiber, 8 g pro.*

SKILLET CHOCOLATE CHIP COOKIE

PREP 20 minutes
BAKE 20 minutes at 350°F

10 Tbsp. unsalted butter
⅔ cup packed light brown sugar
⅓ cup granulated sugar
1 tsp. vanilla
1 egg
1¾ cups all-purpose flour
½ tsp. baking soda
¼ tsp. salt
¾ cup semisweet chocolate chunks

YOU CAN CHANGE UP THE KIND OF CHOCOLATE YOU USE IN THIS GIANT COOKIE. WHITE CHOCOLATE, MILK CHOCOLATE, OR DARK CHOCOLATE PIECES WOULD ALL BE DELICIOUS.

1. Preheat oven to 350°F. In a large heavy oven-going skillet melt butter over medium-low heat; remove skillet from heat. Stir in brown sugar, granulated sugar, and vanilla; cool 5 minutes.
2. Whisk egg into mixture in skillet. Stir in flour, baking soda, and salt until smooth. Quickly stir in chocolate chunks. Press dough into an even layer.

3. Bake 20 to 22 minutes or until cookie is golden brown but center is still soft. Cool in skillet on a wire rack. **MAKES 12 WEDGES.**
PER WEDGE *278 cal., 13 g fat (8 g sat. fat), 41 mg chol., 113 mg sodium, 39 g carb., 1 g fiber, 3 g pro.*

HOT GINGERBREAD COOKIE

PREP 25 minutes

BAKE 18 minutes at 350°F

1 Tbsp. butter, softened

1 cup all-purpose flour

1 tsp. ground ginger

½ tsp. baking soda

¼ tsp. ground cinnamon

¼ tsp. ground cloves

Dash salt

⅓ cup shortening

½ cup sugar

1 egg

2 Tbsp. molasses

4 slices fresh pineapple

1 Tbsp. butter

Caramel ice cream topping (optional)

Cinnamon or butter pecan ice cream

SERVE THIS EASY-TO-MAKE SKILLET COOKIE WITH CARAMELIZED PINEAPPLE PIECES, CARAMEL SAUCE, AND ICE CREAM.

1. Preheat oven to 350°F. Using the softened butter, generously butter a medium heavy oven-going skillet or two individual 10- to 12-oz. skillets, or casseroles. In a bowl stir together the next six ingredients (through salt).

2. In another bowl beat shortening with a mixer on low 30 seconds. Add sugar; beat until combined. Beat in egg and molasses until combined. Beat in as much of the flour mixture as you can with the mixer. Stir in remaining flour mixture. Pour into the prepared skillet(s); spread evenly.

3. Bake until edges of cookie are set. Allow 18 minutes for large skillet or 12 to 14 minutes for small skillets. In another large skillet cook pineapple slices in 1 Tbsp. hot butter over medium-high heat 4 to 5 minutes or until golden brown, turning once.

4. Cool cookie slightly; center will fall slightly. If desired, cut up pineapple. Top cookie with pineapple and, if desired, drizzle with ice cream topping. Serve with ice cream. **MAKES 4 SERVINGS.**

Grilling Directions You need to use a cast-iron skillet(s) or casserole for grilling. Prepare as directed through Step 2, except do not preheat oven. Prepare grill for indirect heat. For a charcoal grill, arrange medium-hot coals around edges of grill, leaving center of grill with no coals. Place skillet(s) in center of grill rack (not over coals). Cover and grill until edges of cookie are set. Allow 15 to 18 minutes for large skillet or 10 to 12 minutes for small skillets. The last 5 to 10 minutes of grilling, add pineapple slices to grill (omit butter), placing them directly over the coals; cover and grill until pineapple is golden brown, turning once. (For a gas grill, preheat grill. Reduce heat to medium. Adjust for indirect grilling. Place skillet(s) over burner that is off. Grill as directed.) Continue as directed in Step 4.

PER SERVING *624 cal., 31 g fat (11 g sat. fat), 81 mg chol., 348 mg sodium, 82 g carb., 2 g fiber, 7 g pro.*

SKILLET BROWNIES

PREP 20 minutes

BAKE 15 minutes at 350°F

1 Tbsp. butter, softened

½ cup butter

3 oz. unsweetened chocolate, coarsely chopped

1 cup sugar

2 eggs

1 tsp. vanilla

⅔ cup all-purpose flour

¼ tsp. baking soda

2 medium bananas

1 Tbsp. butter

Hot fudge ice cream topping (optional)

Ice cream

TOP THESE RICH BROWNIES WITH SAUTÉED BANANAS AND YOUR FAVORITE ICE CREAM. CHOOSE BANANAS THAT ARE RIPE BUT STILL FIRM TO ENSURE THEY DON'T FALL APART IN THE SKILLET.

1. Using the softened butter, generously butter a medium heavy oven-going skillet or four individual 10- to 12-oz. heavy oven-going skillets or casseroles.

2. In a medium saucepan cook and stir the ½ cup butter and the unsweetened chocolate over low heat until melted and smooth. Remove from heat. Stir in sugar. Add eggs, one at a time, beating with a wooden spoon after each addition just until combined. Stir in vanilla. In a bowl stir together flour and baking soda. Add flour mixture to chocolate mixture; stir just until combined. Pour into the prepared skillet(s); spread evenly.

3. Meanwhile, preheat oven to 350°F. Bake brownies just until set in center and edges are firm and pull away from sides. Allow 15 to 20 minutes for large skillet or 20 minutes for small skillets.

4. Peel and slice bananas. In another large skillet cook bananas in 1 Tbsp. butter over medium-high heat 3 to 4 minutes or until golden brown.

5. Top brownies with banana slices, hot fudge topping, if desired, and scoops of ice cream.

MAKES 4 SERVINGS.

Grilling Directions You need to use a cast-iron skillet(s) or casserole for grilling. Prepare as directed through Step 2. For a charcoal grill, arrange medium-hot coals around edges of grill, leaving center of grill with no coals. Place skillet(s) in center of grill rack (not over the coals). Cover and grill just until set in center and edges are firm and pull away from sides. Allow 25 to 30 minutes for large skillet or 20 minutes for small skillets. Meanwhile, cut bananas in half lengthwise. Melt the 1 Tbsp. butter. Brush cut sides of bananas with melted butter. For the last 5 minutes of grilling, add bananas to grill rack directly over coals; grill until lightly browned. (For a gas grill, preheat grill. Reduce heat to medium. Adjust for indirect grilling. Place skillet(s) over burner that is off. Grill as directed.) Remove skillet(s) from grill; let stand 10 minutes. Serve as directed in Step 5.

PER SERVING *873 cal., 51 g fat (30 g sat. fat), 197 mg chol., 369 mg sodium, 106 g carb., 7 g fiber, 11 g pro.*

SKILLET BLONDIES 4 WAYS

PREP **15 minutes**

BAKE **25 minutes at 325°F**

1	Tbsp. butter, softened
	Flour
1½	cups all-purpose flour
½	tsp. baking powder
¼	tsp. salt
¾	cup packed brown sugar
½	cup butter, melted
¼	cup granulated sugar
1	egg
1	tsp. vanilla
¾	cup chopped pecans or walnuts (optional)

KEEP THINGS SIMPLE BY MAKING TRADITIONAL BLONDIES—WITH OR WITHOUT PECANS—OR STIR UP ONE OF FOUR MOUTHWATERING FLAVOR OPTIONS.

1. Preheat oven to 325°F. Using the softened butter, butter and lightly flour a large heavy oven-going skillet. Set aside. In a bowl stir together the flour, baking powder, and salt. In a bowl combine brown sugar, melted butter, and granulated sugar. Whisk egg and vanilla into sugar mixture. Stir in flour mixture just until combined. If desired, stir in pecans.

2. Spread or pat batter into an even layer in skillet. Bake 25* to 30 minutes or until lightly browned and set in the center. Cool in skillet on a wire rack. Loosen edges and invert onto a cutting board. **MAKES 16 WEDGES.**

*Tip Cast-iron skillets retain more heat than stainless-steel or aluminum skillets. Remove after baking 25 minutes.

PER WEDGE *150 cal., 6 g fat (4 g sat. fat), 27 mg chol., 105 mg sodium, 22 g carb., 0 g fiber, 2 g pro.*

WHITE CHOCOLATE-MACADAMIA BLONDIES
Prepare as directed, except omit pecans and stir in ½ cup white chocolate baking pieces and ¼ cup chopped macadamia nuts after stirring in the flour mixture.

PER WEDGE *200 cal., 10 g fat (6 g sat. fat), 7 mg chol., 120 mg sodium, 27 g carb., 0 g fiber, 2 g pro.*

BITTERSWEET CHOCOLATE-ROASTED ALMOND BLONDIES Prepare as directed, except stir in ¼ tsp. almond extract with the vanilla. Omit pecans. Stir in ½ cup chopped bittersweet chocolate and ¼ cup chopped salted roasted almonds after stirring in the flour mixture.

PER WEDGE *192 cal., 9 g fat (5 g sat. fat), 27 mg chol., 116 mg sodium, 26 g carb., 1 g fiber, 2 g pro.*

COCONUT-GRANOLA BLONDIES Prepare as directed, except omit pecans and stir in ½ cup granola and ¼ cup shredded coconut after stirring in the flour mixture.

PER WEDGE *116 cal., 7 g fat (5 g sat. fat), 25 mg chol., 116 mg sodium, 26 g carb., 1 g fiber, 2 g pro.*

CRANBERRY-CLEMENTINE BLONDIES
Prepare as directed, except omit pecans and stir in ⅓ cup coarsely chopped dried cranberries and 1 tsp. clementine zest after stirring in the flour mixture.

PER WEDGE *158 cal., 10 g fat (6 g sat. fat), 27 mg chol., 120 mg sodium, 24 g carb., 0 g fiber, 2 g pro.*

DULCE DE LECHE QUESADILLAS WITH FRUIT SALSA

PREP **20 minutes**

COOK **4 minutes**

1½ cups coarsely chopped fresh pineapple

½ cup fresh blackberries

2 Tbsp. agave nectar or honey

2 tsp. lime juice

Dash salt

4 8-inch flour tortillas

2 Tbsp. unsalted butter, melted

½ cup dulce de leche

1 large banana, sliced

½ cup heavy cream

Dulce de leche

ENJOY THE SWEET SIDE OF QUESADILLAS WITH THIS EASY-TO-MAKE RECIPE. LOOK FOR DULCE DE LECHE—CARAMELIZED SWEETENED CONDENSED MILK—IN THE MEXICAN SECTION OF YOUR SUPERMARKET OR AT MEXICAN FOOD STORES.

1. For fruit salsa, in a bowl combine the first five ingredients (through salt).

2. For quesadillas, lightly brush one side of each tortilla with melted butter. Place tortillas, butter sides down, on cutting board or waxed paper. Using the ½ cup dulce de leche, spread 2 Tbsp. dulce de leche over half of each tortilla. Top with banana slices. Fold tortilla over filling; gently press down.

3. Heat a large nonstick skillet over medium heat for 1 minute. Cook quesadillas, two at a time, in hot skillet 4 to 6 minutes or until lightly browned, turning once. Transfer to cutting board. Cut into wedges.

4. In a bowl beat heavy cream with a mixer on medium until stiff peaks form (tips stand straight). Top quesadilla wedges with fruit salsa and whipped cream. Drizzle with additional dulce de leche. **MAKES 4 SERVINGS.**

PER WEDGE *532 cal., 23 g fat (13 g sat. fat), 68 mg chol., 558 mg sodium, 76 g carb., 3 g fiber, 9 g pro.*

INDEX

METRIC

The charts on this page provide a guide for converting measurements from the U.S. customary system, which is used throughout this book, to the metric system.

PRODUCT DIFFERENCES

Most of the ingredients called for in the recipes in this book are available in most countries. However, some are known by different names. Here are some common American ingredients and their possible counterparts:

- Sugar (white) is granulated, fine granulated, or castor sugar.
- Powdered sugar is icing sugar.
- All-purpose flour is enriched, bleached or unbleached white household flour. When self-rising flour is used in place of all-purpose flour in a recipe that calls for leavening, omit the leavening agent (baking soda or baking powder) and salt.
- Light-color corn syrup is golden syrup.
- Cornstarch is cornflour.
- Baking soda is bicarbonate of soda.
- Vanilla or vanilla extract is vanilla essence.
- Green, red, or yellow sweet peppers are capsicums or bell peppers.
- Golden raisins are sultanas.

VOLUME AND WEIGHT

The United States traditionally uses cup measures for liquid and solid ingredients. The chart below shows the approximate imperial and metric equivalents. If you are accustomed to weighing solid ingredients, the following approximate equivalents will be helpful.

- 1 cup butter, castor sugar, or rice = 8 ounces = ½ pound = 250 grams
- 1 cup flour = 4 ounces = ¼ pound = 125 grams
- 1 cup icing sugar = 5 ounces = 150 grams

Canadian and U.S. volume for a cup measure is 8 fluid ounces (237 ml), but the standard metric equivalent is 250 ml.

1 British imperial cup is 10 fluid ounces.

In Australia, 1 tablespoon equals 20 ml, and there are 4 teaspoons in the Australian tablespoon.

Spoon measures are used for smaller amounts of ingredients. Although the size of the tablespoon varies slightly in different countries, for practical purposes and for recipes in this book, a straight substitution is all that's necessary. Measurements made using cups or spoons always should be level unless stated otherwise.

COMMON WEIGHT RANGE REPLACEMENTS

Imperial / U.S.	Metric
½ ounce	15 g
1 ounce	25 g or 30 g
4 ounces (¼ pound)	115 g or 125 g
8 ounces (½ pound)	225 g or 250 g
16 ounces (1 pound)	450 g or 500 g
1¼ pounds	625 g
1½ pounds	750 g
2 pounds or 2¼ pounds	1,000 g or 1 Kg

OVEN TEMPERATURE EQUIVALENTS

Fahrenheit Setting	Celsius Setting*	Gas Setting
300°F	150°C	Gas Mark 2 (very low)
325°F	160°C	Gas Mark 3 (low)
350°F	180°C	Gas Mark 4 (moderate)
375°F	190°C	Gas Mark 5 (moderate)
400°F	200°C	Gas Mark 6 (hot)
425°F	220°C	Gas Mark 7 (hot)
450°F	230°C	Gas Mark 8 (very hot)
475°F	240°C	Gas Mark 9 (very hot)
500°F	260°C	Gas Mark 10 (extremely hot)
Broil	Broil	Grill

*Electric and gas ovens may be calibrated using celsius. However, for an electric oven, increase celsius setting 10 to 20 degrees when cooking above 160°C. For convection or forced air ovens (gas or electric), lower the temperature setting 25°F/10°C when cooking at all heat levels.

BAKING PAN SIZES

Imperial / U.S.	Metric
9×1½-inch round cake pan	22- or 23×4-cm (1.5 L)
9×1½-inch pie plate	22- or 23×4-cm (1 L)
8×8×2-inch square cake pan	20×5-cm (2 L)
9×9×2-inch square cake pan	22- or 23×4.5-cm (2.5 L)
11×7×1½-inch baking pan	28×17×4-cm (2 L)
2-quart rectangular baking pan	30×19×4.5-cm (3 L)
13×9×2-inch baking pan	34×22×4.5-cm (3.5 L)
15×10×1-inch jelly roll pan	40×25×2-cm
9×5×3-inch loaf pan	23×13×8-cm (2 L)
2-quart casserole	2 L

U.S. / STANDARD METRIC EQUIVALENTS

⅛ teaspoon	= 0.5 ml
¼ teaspoon	= 1 ml
½ teaspoon	= 2 ml
1 teaspoon	= 5 ml
1 tablespoon	= 15 ml
2 tablespoons	= 25 ml
¼ cup = 2 fluid ounces	= 50 ml
⅓ cup = 3 fluid ounces	= 75 ml
½ cup = 4 fluid ounces	= 125 ml
⅔ cup = 5 fluid ounces	= 150 ml
¾ cup = 6 fluid ounces	= 175 ml
1 cup = 8 fluid ounces	= 250 ml
2 cups = 1 pint	= 500 ml
1 quart	= 1 litre